ROYAL ICING

MARY TIPTON &
JOHN WATERHOUSE

Published in 1994 by Merehurst Limited, Ferry House,
51–57 Lacy Road, Putney, London SW15 1PR

Text copyright © Mary Tipton and John Waterhouse 1994
Photography and design copyright © Merehurst Limited 1994

ISBN 1 85391 360 X

Managing Editor Bridget Jones
Edited by Michèle Clarke
Designed by Jo Tapper
Photography by Ken Field
Colour separation by Fotographics Limited, UK-Hong Kong
Printed by Wing King Tong, Hong Kong

The authors and publishers would like to thank the following for their assistance:
Cornish Cakeboards, Rosehill, Goodhavern, Truro, Cornwall TR4 9JT;
Crypto Peerless, Bordesley Green Road, Birmingham B9 1PB; George Wilkinson (Burnley) Ltd.,
Progress Works, Burnley, BB10 1PB; PME (Harrow) Ltd.,
Sugarcraft Division, Brember Road, S. Harrow, Middlesex, HA2 8UN;
Sheila and Ted Seyd and Cornwall College for working space.

NOTES ON USING THE RECIPES
For all recipes, quantities are given in metric, Imperial and cup
measurements. Follow one set of measures only as they are not
interchangeable. Standard 5ml teaspoons (tsp) and 15ml tablespoons
(tbsp) are used. Australian readers, whose tablespoons measure 20ml,
should adjust quantities accordingly. All spoon measures are assumed to
be level unless otherwise stated.
Eggs are a standard size 3 (medium) unless otherwise stated.

CONTENTS

INTRODUCTION

Whilst all sugarcraft skills are individually satisfying, the decorating of celebration cakes is doubly so; this is because the decorator derives pleasure from exercising the special skills of the craft and in addition can share the delight of the person for whom the cake has been made.

Very often customers, or someone to whom a cake has been given, will say that it looks too good to cut. This is a flattering appreciation of our craft but, however exquisite our sugar creation, we must never forget that we are working with food since the purpose of a cake is to be cut and eaten.

Royal icing is enjoying a revival in popularity. This is partly due to technology. Many kitchens now contain an electric food mixer and, together with the widespread availability of dried albumen, this means that correctly aerated icing is easy to achieve and royal icing's 'sweet granite' reputation is being banished. Also, sugarcraft artists appreciate its versatility, the unique skills required in its application and the minimal tools and equipment it requires.

Our aim has been to provide interesting ideas which, whilst seeming complicated, are in fact within the scope of any decorator who has a firm grasp of basic techniques in royal icing. Although some of the designs in this book may appear elaborate, the customer has not been forgotten. Most celebration cakes are cut – and sometimes tiered cakes are assembled – by someone other than the decorator and this needs to be borne in mind by the designer.

There is always demand for unusual ideas and we have used many differing shapes but you do not need a large collection of bakeware; it is possible to hire cake tins (pans) from some kitchenware and sugarcraft shops or, alternatively, the outline can be cut from a simpler shape.

Techniques which have been introduced elsewhere in the Sugarcraft Skills *series – or which the reader may have acquired in classes – are developed further in this book and some simple ideas for using pastillage have been introduced. There is a section on designing your own runout panels and collars as well as a few cakes which are for those occasional orders that offer an opportunity to display skilled technical ability. In addition, because many of those who study for cake decoration and sugarcraft certificates offer their cakes for sale, the relevant aspects of food safety legislation have been referred to.*

Whether your cake decorating is simply for pleasure or strictly vocational we hope you will find some new ideas in these pages and that you will gain satisfaction and enjoyment trying them out.

EQUIPMENT

*T*he equipment required for royal icing work is very simple and in the text it is taken for granted that anyone embarking on intermediate level work will already possess the basics of turntable, straight edge, palette knives, side scraper and some piping tubes (tips), together with an ability to make paper piping bags.

Other equipment referred to specifically in this book includes:

CAKE KNIFE A very sharp knife is essential where cake is to be cut or shaped. For cutting rich fruit cake, a knife with a plain straight blade will give best results.

SIDE SCRAPERS Additional plastic side scrapers which can be cut as required to provide flanges and quick side designs, see Side Designs and Flanges, page 20. A variety of shaped scrapers can also be purchased at cake decorating suppliers.

DOWELS Plastic-covered dowels approved for food use are normally used inside hollow pillars for supporting tiered sugarpasted cakes; they may also be used without pillars for supporting tiered cakes where successive tiers sit directly on the cake beneath.

TILL ROLL/ADDING MACHINE ROLL This inexpensive material available from stationery shops is useful for making templates for cake sides. It is manufactured in a variety of widths and the roll format makes it particularly handy for side templates on large cakes.

STENCIL PAPER This oiled parchment, sold by artists' suppliers, is an excellent medium not only for stencils but also for templates which are required to be used more than once.

SAVOY BAG AND TUBES (TIPS) These large tubes, of metal or polythene, are generally used in pastry work but a 36cm (14 in) nylon savoy bag, kept exclusively for royal icing, and some plain savoy tubes (tips) – 5mm/¼ in, 1cm/½ in, and 2cm/¾ in – will be helpful when creating flanges.

DRAWING EQUIPMENT Some simple drawing equipment will be needed for producing designs for runouts: A3 size sheets of cartridge paper, ruler, HB pencil, pair of compasses, set square, soft pencil eraser, pencil sharpener, and protractor (optional). A flat work surface, such as a drawing board, will make accurate designing easier.

ELECTRIC MIXER A heavy-duty mixing machine with integral stand and a flat beater will take the hard work out of the production of royal icing, leaving you to employ your energies more creatively. It is an essential item for any decorator who plans to decorate cakes in any quantity. If it is fitted with a stainless steel bowl, the machine can also be used for cake mixing and making buttercream. Alternatively, a separate bowl can be purchased and used solely for royal icing to avoid the possibility of contamination of the icing by grease.

MOULDS Some shapes on which to pipe the royal icing net effect will be required, as well as curved shapes, such as plastic guttering, for drying curved runout pieces. Instructions for making your own simple pastillage moulds are given and you are shown how to use simple plastic moulds for pastillage.

In addition to the usual sugarcraft utensils, drawing equipment is essential for drawing precise designs.

*F*or most cake decorators there comes a time when fairly large quantities of icing are required. This may be at a busy season, such as Christmas, or when decorating an extra large or tiered cake. It is assumed that the basic ingredients of royal icing and its making in small quantities and by hand has been covered at introductory level so machine-made royal icing is dealt with here.

A heavy-duty electric mixer with a flat beater will cope easily with a quantity of royal icing which would be difficult to manage by hand; it also saves a considerable amount of time. Check the recommended capacity of your machine and choose whichever of the two royal icing recipes given is most appropriate.

ROYAL ICING

*R*oyal icing is a type of heavy meringue – a mixture of albumen (egg white) and icing (confectioners') sugar. If it is well made it will set firm enough to support tiers yet dissolves in the mouth because it is made up of minute bubbles. The albumen may be provided by fresh egg white but dried hen albumen, fortified powdered albumen or one of the many meringue powders on the market will give more consistent results and avoid any danger of salmonella infection. The dried, or powdered albumen is usually reconstituted in the proportion of 90g(3 oz) albumen to 625ml (20 fl oz/2½ cups) water but always check the manufacturer's instructions.

If you use pure albumen powder reconstitute this according to the manufacturer's instructions (some types require soaking for several hours) and pour the required quantity into the machine bowl.

If you are using a fortified albumen powder, put the measured quantity into the machine bowl, add one third of the required amount of water and gently mix to a smooth consistency with a clean wooden spatula. Add the remaining water and mix.

For general work, if you use a good quality, free-flowing icing (confectioners') sugar, there is no need to sift it before use as the machine will break down any loose lumps. Any icing (confectioners') sugar which contains hard lumps is best avoided.

ROYAL ICING

❖

45g (1½ oz/9 tsp) albumen powder
300ml (10 fl oz/1¼ cups) water
1.6kg (3½ lb) icing (confectioners') sugar
OR
23g (¾ oz/4½ tsp) albumen powder
155ml (5 fl oz/¾ cup) water
875g (1¾ lb/5¼ cups) icing (confectioners') sugar

◯ Ensure that the machine bowl, beater and jug for water are clean and grease-free.

◯ Put one third of the icing (confectioners') sugar into the albumen solution and, using a flat beater not a whisk attachment, mix on the slowest speed until the mixture resembles thin cream. Add a further one third of the icing (confectioners') sugar and continue mixing on the slowest speed. When the sugar is well amalgamated, add the remainder then mix, again on slow speed, for 5 – 7 minutes or until the icing reaches the required consistency.

◯ If the entire batch of royal icing is to be used for one purpose, then mix it to the required

~ 1 ~

FULL PEAK CONSISTENCY *Royal icing beaten to full peak consistency – this will stand straight up when lifted on a spatula or palette knife. This is the consistency for bold piping, flowers, leaves and basket tubes (tips).*

~ 2 ~

COATING CONSISTENCY *Soft peak royal icing for coating – the icing peak droops over from the base.*

~ 3 ~

WRITING AND LINEWORK CONSISTENCY *Royal icing for writing and linework. The consistency is between full peak and soft peak. This is also a good consistency to use for coating where a serrated or comb scraper is used.*

~ 4 ~

RUNOUT CONSISTENCY *Softened royal icing, thinned with a little water or liquid albumen, for runout work.*

consistency. Alternatively, if it is to be used for several purposes – for example, coating, bold piping and linework – mix it to full peak consistency. It is then easier to condition smaller quantities for specific tasks, such as coating.

After mixing, the icing should be scraped down from the sides of the bowl or transferred to a plastic bowl with an airtight lid. The container of royal icing should be covered with a damp cloth whilst in use. Royal icing may be stored in an airtight container and will keep in good condition for about 2 weeks if it is made with dried albumen or fortified albumen powder.

EXPERT ADVICE

≈

If you purchase fortified albumen powder or meringue powder in bulk, first pass the entire contents of the pack through a grease-free, fine mesh sieve before storing. This saves straining the albumen solution each time a batch is made up and will also remove any small hard particles which could spoil coating or block fine piping tubes (tips).It will also help to distribute the starches and albumen more evenly.

REBEATING One feature of royal icing made with fortified albumen powder is that it does not hold its volume for long – left in an airtight bowl overnight it will be found to have 'fallen back' the next day. This is because the albumen content of the powder is only about 50 per cent, the balance being made up of starches and acids which improve the whipping properties. The batch of icing may be scraped into a clean machine bowl and rebeaten for a few minutes on slow speed to renew the volume. Do not be tempted to add additional icing (confectioners') sugar to thicken the icing until it is rebeaten, as this may make the icing heavy. Rebeat first, then decide whether extra sugar is needed.

COLOURING All the coloured cakes illustrated in this book are coated and piped with royal icing tinted with liquid food colouring. If you want to achieve the same colour in successive batches of royal icing then weigh the amount of icing and count the drops of colouring used; keep a note of this for future use. If colour-matching is not important then paste or powder food colourings may be used. To achieve delicate tints, colour a small quantity of royal icing with paste or powder food colouring to a deep tint of that required then add small amounts of this to the main batch of icing, mixing until the desired tint is achieved.

This is a safer way of colouring a large batch of royal icing with paste colour than adding the paste directly to the bulk of the icing.

RUNOUTS

The standard recipe for royal icing may be used for making runouts. Use royal icing of writing consistency for outlines; thin the icing for flooding with liquid albumen (albumen powder reconstituted in water). A special batch of royal icing specifically for runouts may be made up.

30g (1 oz/6 tsp) albumen powder reconstituted in 155ml (5 fl oz/⅔ cup) water
875g (1¾ lb/5¼ cups) icing (confectioners') sugar

~ 1 ~

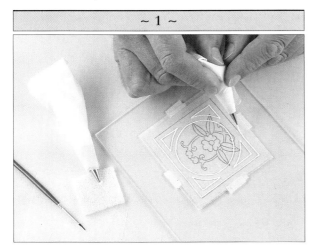

Fix pattern and wax paper to flat surface. Outline runout using no. 1 tube (tip). Where designs include cut-out sections, pipe the inside lines first and work outwards.

~ 2 ~

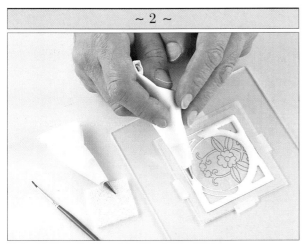

Fill the area to be flooded with run-icing of the required consistency. Use a medium bag cut to the size of a no. 2 tube (tip), or fit a tube.

To use this icing for flooding, thin it with water. Accurate drawing or copying of patterns for runout sections and collars is important, otherwise the finished pieces will not fit the cake. Make sure that patterns are completely flat and that the paper used to pipe on is crease-free. This paper may be wax paper, cellophane or a specially-treated mat which is re-usable and designed specifically for runout work.

For flat pieces the consistency of the run-icing should be that shown on page 9, Royal Icing Consistencies. For pieces with narrow sections or for curved runouts, a thicker icing will be required.

Dry each runout piece quickly near a gentle heat source, such as an angled desk lamp, and leave dried runouts on the wax paper until you are ready to use them. Store runouts in a warm, dry place.

STENCILS

Stencils provide a speedy method for adding inscriptions to cakes, producing accurate repeat designs quickly and for making simple motifs, such as petals, hearts, bells and butterflies.

A wide selection of commercial stencils are available, made in metal, acetate or stencil paper. With care, you can cut your own designs using acetate or stencil paper.

To stencil directly on the cake surface, fix the stencil carefully in place with masking tape or press firmly in place with thumb and forefinger. Using a narrow-bladed palette knife spread the royal icing across the cut-out area, spreading away from thumb and finger. Remove the stencil taking care not to disturb the icing.

Curved stencil shapes can be produced by

~ 1 ~

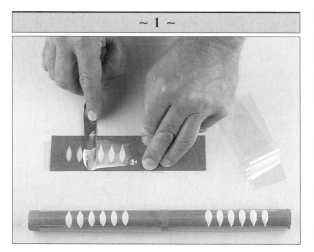

FLOWERS Hold a petal pattern stencil in position firmly at one end. Spread the royal icing away from that end. Remove stencil carefully, place paper over or. inside a curved former to dry, depending on the effect desired. Make leaves in a similar fashion, using green royal icing.

~ 2 ~

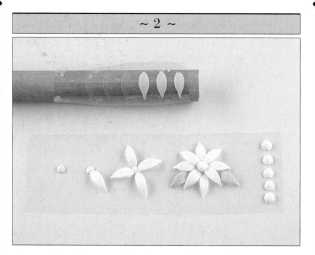

Assemble dry petals into a flower by piping a bulb of icing onto a square of wax paper and arrange the petals in it. For centres, pipe bulbs of icing onto wax paper using a no. 2 tube (tip); dust with caster (superfine) sugar. When dry, fix flower centre in place with a dot of icing.

stencilling onto wax paper and placing the paper over or inside a curved former to dry. This method can be used to make flowers and leaves. This method is quicker than making runout shapes and thinner petals can be made in this way.

PASTILLAGE

*A*ny sugar paste which contains a setting agent is a form of pastillage. Recipes vary but usually powdered gelatine and /or gum tragacanth are used to make the paste set firm.

The various pastes can then be used for making models, display pieces, flowers, plaques and ornaments.Pastillage is a material which works very well with royal icing because, uncoloured, it is the same sparkling white and the surface texture is similar to that of royal icing.

Knead the pastillage well before use. As it dries very quickly when exposed to air, keep well wrapped when not in use.

If pastillage is to be used as part of the decoration fixed to a cake, as in the acanthus leaves on the Old Fashioned Wedding Cake (p.32), mix it 50:50 with sugarpaste otherwise it will set so hard that it will be difficult to cut and impossible to eat.

Avoid rolling out pastillage on a stainless steel surface – this is cold and the pastillage will start to set whilst it is being rolled out.

EXPERT ADVICE

≈

Chocolate and marzipan moulds can be used for modelling pastillage

---

~ 1 ~

PLAQUES AND FLAT PIECES *Roll out pastillage to required thickness on a surface lightly dusted with cornflour (cornstarch). Turn over, placing large pieces on drying board before cutting. Use a scalpel for cutting round templates. Dry on cellophane-covered board or unpolished wood.*

~ 2 ~

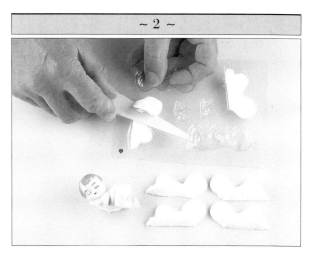

Dust kneaded pastillage lightly with cornflour (cornstarch); press into mould. Trim from centre towards edges. Turn out and re-knead; re-mould this paste, now trimmed to exact amount. Unmould and dry. Press two-part models together, then dry.

~ 3 ~

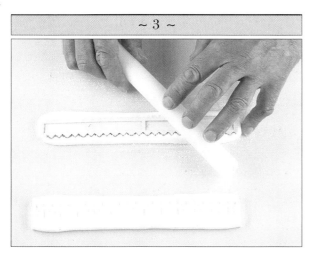

To make your own mould, knead pastillage until smooth. Form into approximate shape of object to be reproduced. Dust lightly with cornflour and press master shape in evenly and firmly. Run rolling pin over back to level. Remove master and allow to set.

~ 4 ~

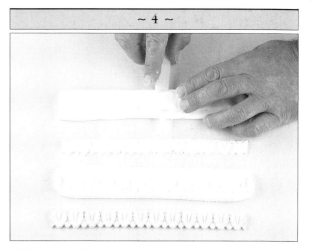

When pastillage is hard, use as in step 2 but trim excess using a marzipan knife or thin-bladed palette knife not a sharp knife which will dig into mould. If 50:50 pastillage/ sugarpaste is used, fix to the cake immediately after moulding. Overpipe when crusted.

PASTILLAGE

❖

500g (1 lb/3 cups) icing (confectioners') sugar
30g (1 oz/3 tbsp) cornflour (cornstarch)
10g (⅓ oz/2 tsp) powdered gelatine
60ml (2 fl oz/¼ cup) cold water
30g (1 oz) Royal Icing, see page 8

⦿ Sift together the icing (confectioners') sugar and cornflour (cornstarch). Heat to 70°C (150° F) in a heatproof bowl over a pan of water. Sprinkle gelatine over cold water in a small heatproof bowl. Leave to soften for 2 – 3 minutes until sponged. Stand bowl over a saucepan of hot water. Do not allow water to boil. Stir gelatine until dissolved.

⦿ Add dissolved gelatine to dry ingredients and mix to a smooth, dry paste. Work in royal icing; knead well. Double wrap tightly in polythene bags; store in covered container.

EXPERT ADVICE

≈

To ensure an even, fine coating of cornflour (cornstarch) on pastillage for moulding, make a dusting bag of muslin (cheesecloth) or other fine material.

SHAPED CAKES

*C*akes other than the familiar round and square in shape can offer a challenge to the cake decorator willing to experiment. Shaped cakes are also a way of expanding your portfolio of designs.

Many different shapes of baking tin are now available – we have used oval, petal, heart, hexagonal, scalloped oval, as well as round and square. Sometimes other utensils can, if suitably lined, be used for baking a cake, for example a pudding basin or roasting tin (pan), see Welcome Baby cake, page 38. Round and square shapes can be 'disguised' with runout panels so that they appear to be a more interesting shape. Good quality tins (pans) may be hired from some kitchenware and sugarcraft shops if storage space is at a premium or you want to try out a particular shape before investing in your own tins (pans).

Calculating the quantity of cake mixture required for shaped tins (pans) and frames can be a problem. If you take a tin (pan) you use regularly and pour in water to the usual level of your mixture, then pour that water into the

---

EXPERT ADVICE

≈

Numeral-shaped tins (pans) are usually made as baking frames, that is they have no base and must be placed on a baking sheet. Whenever possible, reverse a numeral frame before lining and filling with cake mixture then when it is baked and upturned you will have a flat top to the cake.

~ 1 ~

To obtain neat, sharp edges on straight-sided cakes, coat opposite or alternate sides in royal icing. Allow to dry, then coat the remaining sides. Allow to dry, then coat the top. Repeat the process until three coats have been applied to all surfaces.

~ 2 ~

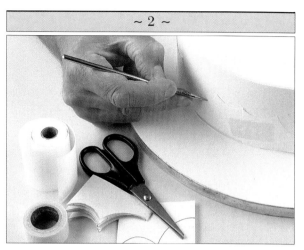

Till roll/adding machine roll is ideal for side templates. Unwind the roll around the cake, mark and cut the required length, then fold the strip into the number of sections required. Draw the shape and cut with sharp scissors. Hold template in place with a piece of masking tape.

~ 3 ~

When a design calls for a deep cake this is best achieved by joining two cakes of standard depth. Brush the tops of both cakes with boiled apricot purée and marzipan (almond paste) in the usual way. Brush the base of one cake with boiled apricot purée and fix in place on top.

~ 4 ~

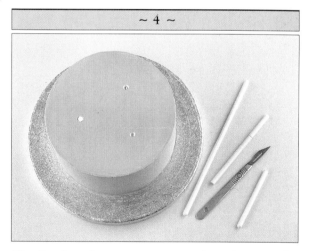

To fix dowels to support another tier or solid pillars, decide on the position of the dowels and mark. Push on dowel straight into cake and mark height. Cut all dowels to this length, using a sharp knife. Push dowels into position.

shaped tin (pan) you will have a guide to the quantity of mixture required. To measure the volume of a frame, stand it on a baking sheet and line it with a polythene bag.

A tiered caked may include two or more different shapes and this idea will open up many design possibilities. If the individual cakes in a tiered design are required to be of different depths, a way of achieving this without wastage is to interline the cake tin (pan) with a plain band of greaseproof (parchment) or non-stick paper cut to the requisite depth. Fill the tin (pan) with cake mixture to the level of this inner band.

When the only way to achieve the required shape is to cut a cake, the trimmings need not be wasted. If large enough, they can be cut neatly and given to customers as samples; smaller trimmings can be stored in a polythene bag in the freezer until you have sufficient to use for truffles, see page 17, or any other recipe for leftovers.

MARZIPAN (ALMOND PASTE) COATING

A clean, sharp edge where top and sides meet, and at angles, such as the top and bottom of a heart shape, is as important on shaped cakes as it is on round or square cakes which are prepared for royal icing. Achieving this sharpness means covering the top and sides separately, and often involves cutting separate sections for each of the sides, as you would for a square cake – six sections for a hexagonal cake, eight for octagonal, and so on. The sides of a heart cake are best covered with two separate pieces of marzipan (almond paste).

Coating straight-sided cakes is shown in the steps on page 15. Coating the sides of curved shapes can also be done in separate stages.

HEART SHAPE Coat in two stages, each commencing at one side of the upper V and finishing at the lower V.

PETAL SHAPE Can be coated in one operation, carefully taking the side scraper round each scallop but a cleaner finish will be achieved by coating alternate scallops; allow them to dry then coat the remaining scallops.

SCALLOPED OVAL May be coated as the petal shape.

HORSESHOE SHAPE Is the most difficult shape to coat. The outside and end pieces are relatively straightforward but care is needed to achieve a neat finish on the inner curve. An upright palette knife will be found to be the most useful tool for this task.

DOWELS

Not all celebration cakes are made from rich fruit cake; some customers may prefer a light fruit or a madiera base. These can be covered in marzipan (almond paste) and coated in exactly the same way as a rich fruit cake but in some designs this type of base may not support the upper tiers. Here dowels may be used to act as supports.

Food-quality plastic dowels may be cut level with or slightly higher than the top of the cake coating. The upper tier will then rest on the dowels, not on the lower tier so there is no danger of the tiers sinking. First check that your cake is level. If not, select the dowel position at the highest point of the cake surface, push in a dowel down to the board and mark the height. Cut all dowels to this length. Save the excess dowel pieces for another cake or for use as spacers for raised runouts, see Anniversary Cake, page 62.

PACKAGING AND DELIVERY
❖

Multi-tiered cakes are best finally assembled after delivery as securing all tiers in position for transporting could be difficult and time-consuming. Besides, caterers who are to cut and portion the cake will want easy access to each tier.

Packaging cakes which are to be assembled with pillars is not difficult but to be sure that the cake is assembled as you designed it, indicate the position of the pillars on each tier, perhaps by outlining them with a piped line of royal icing, and, if pillars of different heights are used, indicate which pillars belong to which tier.

Cakes designed so that each tier sits directly on the tier below it, present more of a problem. Usually the upper tiers will be set on thin boards which may be iced over so as to be invisible. This tier may be positioned with the aid of a crank-handled palette knife or, if the side design permits, grasped between fingers and thumb of each hand and carefully lowered into place. Since there is no splay of board to protect the side decorations care is needed in packaging. The cake may be set on a layer of thin foam sponge on a board which fits the delivery box snugly. This should prevent movement, and subsequent damage, during transport.

EXPERT ADVICE
≈

Cutting rich fruit cake after the celebration cut has been made is best done with a plain, straight-bladed knife, such as a carving knife, rather than a chef's knife or serrated blade. Make sure the knife is very sharp. Use a smooth, sawing motion without pressing down and wipe the blade clean after each cut to remove traces of marzipan which will quickly dry on the blade and will cause the cake to drag and crumble. Cut straight through the centre of the cake, remove half to a cutting board then cut slices of the required thickness. Cut each slice into fingers for serving.

RICH TRUFFLES
❖

If you have any cake trimmings left over, here is a delicious way to use them up.

300g (12 oz) cake trimmings, crumbled
100g (4 oz/¼ lb) chocolate chips, melted
60ml (2 fl oz/¼ cup) golden syrup
(light corn syrup)
2 tbsp brandy
60ml (2 fl oz/¼ cup) whisky or dark rum
icing (confectioners') sugar for dredging

Combine all ingredients, except icing (confectioners') sugar, and mix well. Roll small amounts of the mixture in your hands to form balls. Roll balls in icing sugar (confectioners') sugar and refrigerate to harden.

ENGAGEMENT CAKE

*T*he slanting top of this cake is an ideal surface for an elegant monogram, making it a design suitable for engagements, weddings or anniversaries.

13cm (5 in) heart cake
20cm (8 in) petal cake
apricot glaze
1kg (2¼ lb) marzipan (almond paste)
1.5kg (3 lb) Royal Icing, see page 8
pale green food colouring
3 dowels (optional)
EQUIPMENT
14cm (5½ in) heart cake card
30cm (12 in) petal board
33cm (13 in) petal board
non-toxic adhesive
tracing paper
stencil paper
scriber
no. 0, 1, 2, 3, 43 and 44 piping tubes (tips)
about 2m (2¼ yd) ribbon or paper banding for board edge

Cut the heart-shaped cake as shown on page 21. Brush both cakes with apricot glaze and cover with marzipan (almond paste) as described on page 16. Place the heart-shaped cake on the cake card and support on a smaller board whilst you coat and decorate the cake.

Using non-toxic adhesive stick the two petal-shaped boards together. Centre the petal-shaped cake on the upper board.

Coat the cakes with pale green coloured royal icing, leaving some icing uncoloured for the decoration. Coat the splay on the petal-shaped boards when the final coat of icing is completed. Leave to dry. Fix dowels into the petal-shaped cake if wished, see page 16.

Trace appropriate letters for the monogram using the enlarged alphabet from page 66 and scribe onto cake top. Pipe using no.2 and 1 tubes (tips) and white royal icing.

Pipe grape clusters on the sides of the petal cake, as shown in step-by-step instructions on page 21. Pipe the vertical line with a no.2 tube (tip), overpiped with no.1 in green royal icing. Overpipe with white icing and no.1 tube (tip). Pipe scratched-line scallop using no.0 tube (tip) and white icing.

BORDERS: HEART CAKE Divide the top and base borders into six. On the top, using pale green royal icing, pipe 'C' scrolls on the left, reverse 'C' scrolls on the right with no.43 tube (tip) and a roping motion. Overpipe with similar scrolls. Using a no.2 tube (tip) and white icing, overpipe with a small plain shell.

At the base, using pale green icing and no.43 tube, pipe a roped 'C' scroll and reverse 'C' scroll on each side, as for the top border. Overpipe as for top border. Pipe a leaf at the base of each scroll, using white royal icing and a piping bag cut to a 'V' shape. Emphasize the shape of the scrolls with a scalloped line using a no.1 tube (tip) and white icing.

On the cake top, pipe a scalloped line inside the scrolls, using white royal icing and no.1 tube (tip).

BORDERS: PETAL CAKE Using pale green icing and no.44 tube (tip), pipe a 'C' scroll and reverse 'C' scroll on each scallop. Overpipe with similar scrolls. Overpipe with a small, plain shell using no.3 tube (tip) and pale green icing. Overpipe with plain shells twice more, using

white icing and no.2 tube (tip) followed by no.1 tube (tip).

● On top of the petal cake, pipe built-up linework in pale green royal icing. The first row is piped with no.3 tube (tip) overpiped with no.2 then no.1 tube (tip). The second row is piped using no.2 then no.1 tube (tip). A third row is piped inside these using a no.1 tube (tip) and white icing. Finally, using a no.1 tube (tip) and white royal icing, pipe a scratched-line scallop inside the linework, and round the edge of the two petal cake boards.

● Fix the ribbon trim round the petal cake boards, then pipe a row of bulbs between the upper and lower boards using white royal icing and a no.3 tube (tip).

● To assemble, the heart cake is placed centrally on top of the petal cake.

EXPERT ADVICE

≈

If you are nervous about piping directly on the cake side, the grape clusters may be piped on wax paper. When completely dry, the grapes may be attached to the cake with a little royal icing.

SIDE DESIGNS AND FLANGES

*B*ecause the emphasis is usually on the top decoration of a celebration cake the sides can sometimes be neglected. Shaped scrapers can be used to good effect to provide side interest without too much effort. They are available in plastic or metal in a variety of configurations, the most common being the comb or serrated scraper which is often used with buttercream or chocolate in the decoration of gâteaux and fancies. You can give your work an individual touch by cutting your own design from a plain plastic scraper.

The shaped scraper is used on the final coat of icing. The icing must be paddled on to at least the thickness of the deepest indentation in the design; a firmer icing is best for this with the consistency between full peak and soft peak. The scraper is employed in the normal way to smooth the sides but since the icing is of a deeper-than-usual thickness more excess is scraped away – care must be taken not to overload the scraper. If necessary, reposition the scraper carefully and take it round the cake sides a second time for an even finish. This technique can also be used on an iced splay on the cake board.

STRIPED ICING A comb scraper may be used to create a striped effect. This is achieved by coating the cake side with a deep shade of icing and allowing this to dry. Then a paler coating is applied and a comb scraper used to mark the stripes, as shown on page 22. It is important that the ends of the teeth are filed flat.

continued on page 22

~ 1 ~

To cut cake at a slant measure side, in this case from upper 'V' to lower 'V'. Cut two templates this length, tapering from 6.5cm (2½ in) to 2.5cm (1 in). Fix to cake with wooden cocktail sticks (toothpicks). Using a very sharp knife, saw away excess cake above line of template.

~ 2 ~

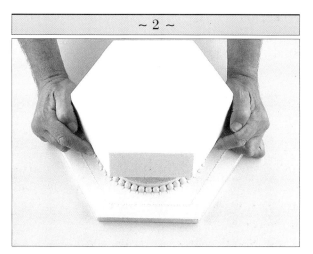

Where a design calls for the cake board to remain invisible, place the cake on a slightly larger card then marzipan (almond paste) and coat with the card in place. Position cake on smaller board or upturned bowl whilst decorating,

~ 3 ~

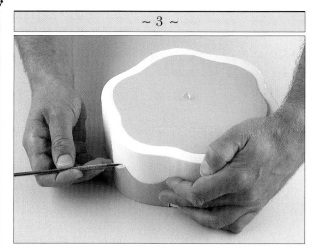

Stencil paper (oiled parchment) is ideal for templates which are to be used more than once. Here it is used as a guide for scribing a design on a multi-sided cake and is shown cut as a template for top linework.

~ 4 ~

Bunches of grapes may be piped directly onto the cake surface. Start with a shell shape then cover it with small plain bulbs piped in random fashion to represent grapes. Finish with vine leaves piped using a bag cut to an inverted 'V'.

~ ❖ ~

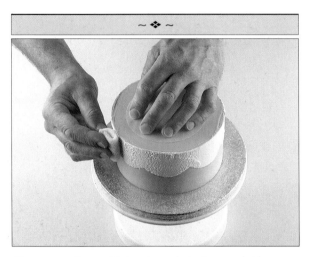

STIPPLED ICING Cut a template to mask the area which is to remain smooth, hold or fix in place and spread royal icing over the exposed section with a palette knife. After about 10 minutes use a piece of foam sponge to stipple the icing. Remove the template and dry.

~ ❖ ~

This effect of striped icing is achieved by using a comb scraper with the ends of the teeth flattened. Coat the side in a deep shade; when dry apply a coat of paler icing, then use the comb scraper.

STIPPLED ICING Small areas of stippled icing can add interesting texture on a cake. This is applied to a dry base coat, using a template to mask areas which are to remain smooth. The icing is allowed to set for about 10 minutes before the texure is imposed on it by using a piece of foam sponge. Dab the icing lightly and evenly as shown in the step picture, left.

FLANGES
❖

Flanges provide bolder designs and can give a better balanced appearance to the base border, especially on large or deep cakes. It will be easiest to cut the flange design yourself as its position on the cake side will be dictated by the depth of the cake.

Cut the design in plastic scrapers, as shown in step 1, right. It is important to make sure you achieve a smooth edge on the cut to give a good finish on the icing. The steps show two alternative flanges made using specially cut scrapers: the first is applied around the middle of the cake, the second creates a neat finish between the cake base and the board.

Both side and base flanges are applied after the final coat of icing and the technique is shown in the step-by-step illustrations, see opposite. They provide an excellent base on which to display side piping or built-up borders.

~ 1 ~

Cut your own designs in plastic scrapers using a heavy-duty hole punch, metal file, sharp craft knife or hot metal skewer. Rub down any rough edges with fine sandpaper. Using the scraper as a guide, scribe a line round centre of cake.

~ 2 ~

Pipe a line of icing along this, using a plain savoy tube and bag. The icing needs to be full peak consistency.

~ 3 ~

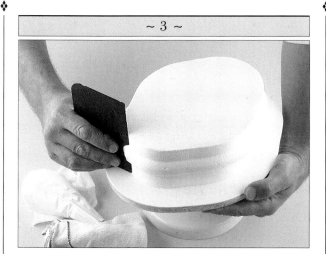

Take the shaped scraper round the cake to leave the bold flange in place. Allow to dry.

~ 4 ~

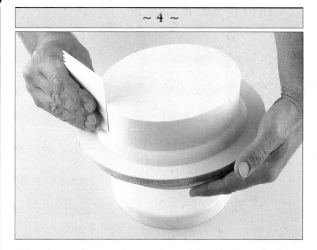

The base flange is produced in similar fashion when cake and board coating have dried. Pipe a bold line at the base of the cake then neaten with cut scraper. Allow to dry.

CHRISTMAS CAKE

*A*side flange has been used to emphasize the shape of the scalloped oval cake with its elegant runout sleigh and frosty icicles and snowballs.

20 x 15cm (8 x 6 in) scalloped oval cake
apricot glaze
750g (1½ lb) marzipan (almond paste)
750g (1½ lb) Royal Icing, see page 8
red and green food colourings
caster (superfine) sugar for dredging
E Q U I P M E N T
30 x 25cm (12 x 10 in) scalloped oval
cake board
shaped sidescraper
tracing paper
A4 sheet cartridge paper
wax paper
no. 1, 2 and 3 piping tubes (tips)
about 1m (1¼ yd) ribbon for cake
about 1m (1¼ yd) ribbon or paper banding for
board edge

Brush the cake with apricot glaze and cover with marzipan (almond paste) as described on page 16. Coat the cake with white royal icing. Following the step-by-step instructions on page 20, for side designs and flanges, make a centre flange round the cake sides. Coat the cake board. Leave to dry.

Pipe the icicles following the instructions on page 26.

Using a no.3 tube (tip) and white royal icing, pipe bulbs at the base border. Pipe similar bulbs at the top border but leave space between each bulb for a further bulb to be piped. Dredge all these piped bulbs with caster (superfine) sugar. Allow to dry, then brush away excess sugar. Pipe bulbs between the existing bulbs on the top edge.

Following the instructions on page 26, make sugar bells.

Pipe plain shells around the base of the flange using no.2 tube (tip) and white royal icing.

Trace the runout sleigh pieces using the pattern on page 68. Make the runout sections following the instructions on page 10. Use liquid or powder colouring to achieve the deep red colour; the glycerine in paste colour will prevent the runout drying.

Using the pattern on page 68, trace the sleigh linework and scribe onto the cake top. Pipe the linework using a no.1 tube (tip), first in white royal icing then overpipe in green.

Pipe the decoration on the runout pieces using white royal icing and a no.1 tube (tip). When dry, position runout pieces on cake top, fixing with a few dots of white royal icing.

Dab white royal icing underneath the sleigh runners to represent snow. Pipe the single line inside the top border on the cake using a no.3 tube (tip) and white royal icing. Note that it does not form a complete circle. Attach sugar bells at the end of the line as illustrated.

Pipe quick holly and berries onto the plain bulbs on the top border and round the edge of the cake board, following the step-by-step instructions on page 26.

Fix ribbon round centre of flange, using small bulbs of royal icing at the joins in the curves. Fix sugar bells with small bulbs of icing and pipe quick holly and berries.

Trim the board edge with ribbon or paper banding.

~ 1 ~

When the flange is dry, pipe the icicles at the top edge of the cake using a no.2 tube (tip) and white royal icing. Dredge caster (superfine) sugar over, before they begin to crust (see Expert Advice box). When dry, brush excess sugar away

EXPERT ADVICE

≈

When dredging sections of a cake with caster (superfine) sugar, first remove it from the decorating area to prevent sugar crystals from getting into the batch of royal icing.

~ 2 ~

BELLS Using a no.3 tube, pipe a tapered bulb on top of a flat bulb on wax paper. Dredge with caster (superfine) sugar at once. When the outer surface has crusted, gently scoop out the soft centre with a cocktail stick (toothpick) or paintbrush. Leave to dry.

~ 3 ~

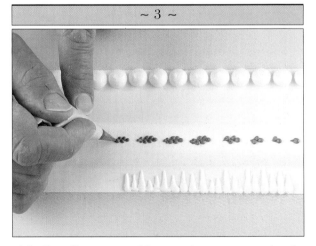

A holly effect is quickly piped using a no.1 tube (tip) and green royal icing. Pipe small plain shells in the shape of a holly leaf, as shown. Pipe tiny red dots for berries, using a no.1 tube (tip).

KEEPSAKE CAKE

This ideal gift for Mother is also the answer for the person who thinks a cake looks too nice to eat – a pastillage cake top which can be kept whilst the cake itself is cut and eaten.

20cm (8 in) round cake
apricot glaze
1kg (2 lb) marzipan (almond paste)
875g (1¾ lb) Royal Icing, see page 8
selection of food colourings
18cm (7 in) round pastillage plaque
6 large piped roses
4 medium piped roses
14 piped rosebuds
EQUIPMENT
30cm (12 in) round cake board
shaped side scraper
tracing paper
scriber
no. 1, 2, 3 and 32R piping tubes (tips)
about 1m (1¼ yd) ribbon or paper banding for board edge

Brush the cake with apricot glaze and cover with marzipan (almond paste). Coat the cake with pale apricot coloured royal icing, leaving some uncoloured royal icing for the decoration. Use the shaped scraper for the final coat on the side of the cake (see Side Designs and Flanges, page 20). Coat the splay on the board when the final coat of icing is completed. Leave to dry.

Using no.3 tube (tip) and pale apricot coloured royal icing, pipe bulb borders at top and base. Overpipe with a continuous line piped off-centre, first with no.3 then no.2 and no.1 tubes (tips). With a no.1 tube (tip) and deeper apricot royal icing, overpipe with a final line, then pipe a small, plain, deep apricot shell at each join in the linework on the top border.

Pipe the basket onto the pastillage plaque, following the step-by-step instructions on page 30. Using a no.2 tube (tip) and pale apricot coloured royal icing, pipe a plain shell border to the plaque.

Using deep apricot coloured royal icing, pipe the slotted-ribbon effect between the ridges on the cake side, as shown on page 30. Finish with an icing bow at front of cake. Pipe a ribbon bow on basket handle.

Fix the piped roses and buds in position on plaque using small bulbs of icing. Pipe green leaves amongst roses, using a small piping bag cut to a 'V' at the end.

Attach the plaque to the cake top with just two or three small bulbs of icing, so that it can be removed easily.

Trim board edge with ribbon or paper banding.

EXPERT ADVICE

≈

Petal tubes are available for both right- and left-handed users. The instructions given are for right-handed use. If you are using a left-handed tube just reverse the instructions, i.e. read left for right and clockwise for counter-clockwise. Straight petal tubes are also available which are suitable for right- or left-handed operation.

~ 1 ~

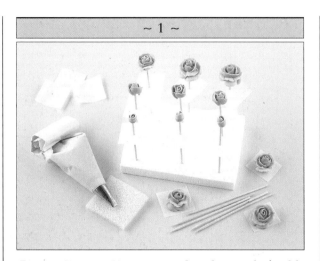

PIPED ROSES *Use a petal tube and freshly beaten full peak icing. Push a cocktail stick (toothpick) through wax paper. Hold tube at right angles to stick, wide end down and narrow end inward. Turn stick counter-clockwise while piping bud by dropping tube slightly.*

~ 2 ~

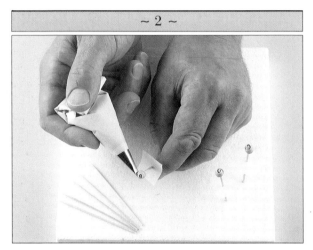

Pipe three or four tiny overlapping petals round bud. Turn stick counter-clockwise using an up-and-down motion. Pipe a further five overlapping petals in the same way, tucking wide end of tube (tip) beneath second row to give shape to flower.

~ 3 ~

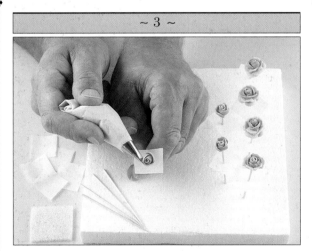

Finish with five overlapping petals piped counter-clockwise so petals appear to be opening. Slide wax paper up to remove flower.

~ 4 ~

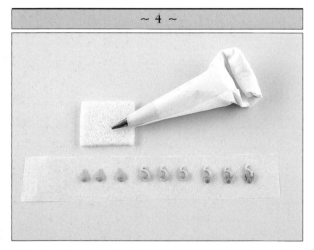

Flat buds are piped on wax paper using plain tubes (tips). Start with a tear-drop shape then pipe an 'S' shape down it. Finish with green calyx and rose hip.

~ 1 ~

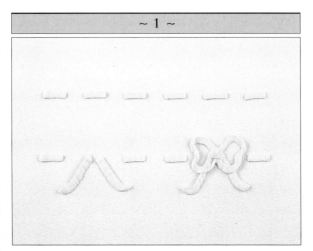

Using a no.32R tube (tip) pipe short lengths of icing at intervals to represent slotted ribbon. The piping tube is held at an angle of about 45° with the end at right angles to you. The ribbon effect can be completed with an icing bow.

~ 2 ~

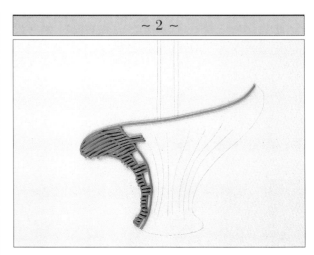

Trace the basket template on page 31 and scribe onto the pastillage plaque. Using a no.2 tube (tip) and brown royal icing, pipe the top and left-hand side and the first upright as shown. Pipe the horizontal lines across the uprights in a series of three lines, ending at the scribed line for the second upright. Pipe the next horizontal row in three lines from the basket edge to the first upright.

~ 3 ~

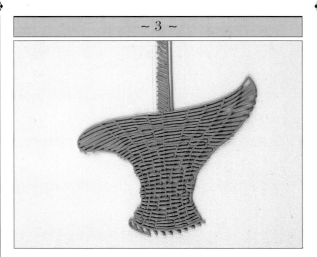

Pipe from top to bottom of the basket in alternating rows in this fashion. Pipe the next upright and continue piping horizontal lines as in step 2. Complete by piping base and handle.

EXPERT ADVICE

≈

Follow the instructions for piping the ribbon and bow, step 1, when piping the bow on the top of the basket handle before arranging the roses in position.

Basket Template

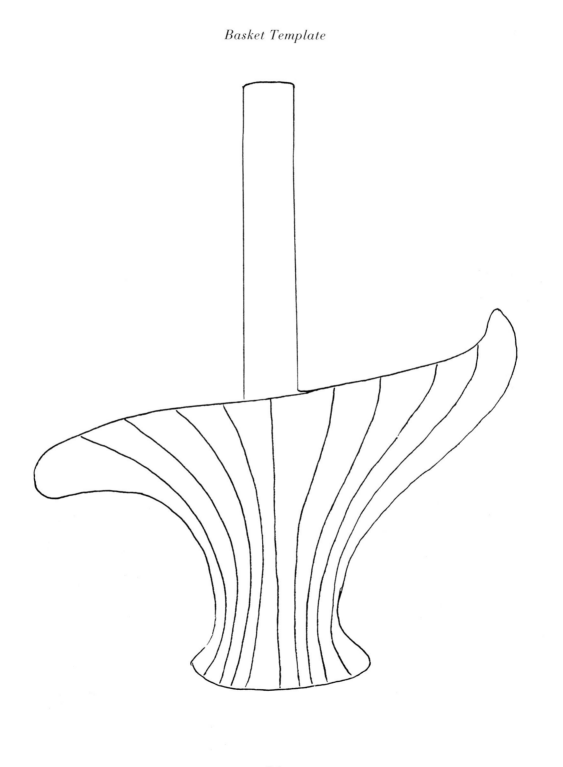

OLD-FASHIONED WEDDING CAKE

*T*he richness of Edwardian times is echoed in this two-tier oval cake which is deceptively simple to decorate using soft pastillage moulding.

25 x 20cm (10 x 8 in) oval cake
15 x 10cm (6 x 4 in) oval cake
apricot glaze
2kg (4 lb) marzipan (almond paste)
2kg (4 lb) Royal Icing, see page 8
cream food colouring
250g (8 oz) pastillage mixed with 250g (8 oz)
sugarpaste

EQUIPMENT

36 x 30cm (14 x 12 in) oval cake board
38 x 33cm (15 x 13 in) oval cake board
non-toxic adhesive
25 x 20cm (10 x 8 in) oval cake board
shaped side scraper
border mould, see page 13
tracing paper
scriber
no. 1, 3, 43 and 44 piping tubes (tips)
about 2m (2¾ yd) ribbon or paper banding for board edge
three 5cm (2 in) cream-coloured pillars

Brush the cakes with apricot glaze and cover with marzipan (almond paste). Using non-toxic adhesive, bond the two larger cake boards together. Position the cakes on their respective boards and coat with pale cream-coloured royal icing, using a deeper cream icing for the final coat on the top of each cake. Coat the boards when the final coat of icing is completed. Leave to dry.

Following the step-by-step instructions on page 23 for Side Designs and Flanges, make base flanges around both cakes. Leave to dry.

Colour the mixed pastillage and sugarpaste pale cream and use it to make lengths of moulding, as shown in the step-by-step instructions on page 13. Fix these to the cake sides using royal icing, around the top edge and above the flange. On the bottom tier, fix lengths of moulding around the upper board, curving the top edge over the board if necessary.

Trace the templates for the cake tops from the design on page 71 and scribe onto the cakes.

Pipe the top linework on both tiers following the line drawings on page 71 and using the close-up photographs on page 34 for reference.

BOTTOM TIER: For the top border, mark the top edge of the cake with a dot of royal icing opposite each point of the linework, to give two short sections at each end and two longer sections on each side. Using a no.44 tube (tip), pipe a tapered rope scroll in each section. Overpipe with a repeated tapered rope scroll. Overpipe with plain shells using a no.3 piping tube (tip). With deeper cream icing, overpipe with another row of plain shells, using a no.2 tube (tip).

Midway around the side of the cake, mark points immediately beneath the joins in the top border. Pipe overpiped tapered rope scrolls in each division following the same sequence as for the top border. Using a no.3 tube (tip) pipe a bulb at each join and a fleur-de-lys shape above.

Using a no.43 tube (tip) pipe upright shells around the base of the flange. Pipe a small bulb at the point of each using deep cream icing and a no.1 tube.

~ 1 ~

Pipe the linework on the cake tops using this photograph as a guide.

~ 2 ~

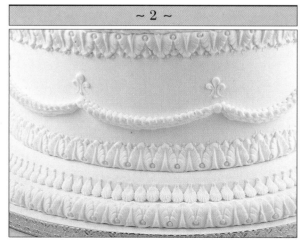

The piped embellishment on the moulding is shown here. Use deep cream royal icing and a no.1 piping tube (tip).

TOP TIER: Divide the top edge of the cake in the same fashion as for the bottom tier. Pipe a tapered rope scroll in each section using a no.43 tube (tip). Overpipe with plain shells twice, first with a no.3 tube (tip) and then with deeper cream icing and a no.2 tube (tip)

● Using a no.42 tube (tip), pipe upright shells round the base of the flange. Pipe a small dot of deep cream icing at the point of each shell, using a no.1 tube (tip).

● On both cakes, overpipe the moulded decoration with bulbs and shell shapes in deep cream icing, using a no.1 tube (tip), and using the close-up photograph, bottom left, as a reference.

● Trim the board edges with ribbon or paper banding.

EXPERT ADVICE

≈

Traditional wedding cakes supported by pillars are sometimes displayed on a table where the undersides of the upper tier boards are visible to seated guests. For a professional finish stick a thin silver cake card, of the same size as the cake board, to the base of the board, silver side out, or cut coloured paper to shape and cover the bottom of the boards with this to enhance any colour theme that has been used.

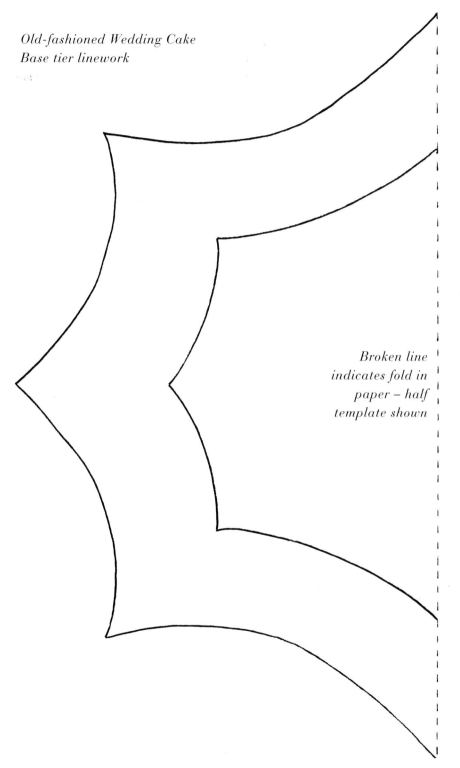

Old-fashioned Wedding Cake
Base tier linework

Broken line
indicates fold in
paper – half
template shown

WELCOME BABY

The Christening or naming of a baby is always a cause for celebration. Custom has been broken here by the use of yellow to highlight the traditional blue for a boy but the design is easily adapted for a baby girl or you could use other colours of your choice.

25 x 20cm (10 x 8 in) cake
apricot glaze
1kg (2 lb) marzipan (almond paste)
boiled water or clear alcohol (kirsch or vodka)
1kg (2 lb) sugarpaste
500g (1 lb) Royal Icing, see page 8
blue and yellow food colourings
sleeping babe ornament
EQUIPMENT
25 x 20cm (10 x 8 in) oblong cake card
30 x 25cm (12 x 10 in) oblong cake board
scriber
tracing paper
no.1 and 57 piping tubes (tips)

● Brush the cake with apricot glaze and cover with marzipan (almond paste). Brush with cooled boiled water or alcohol and cover with sugarpaste. Centre the cake on the cake card and support on a smaller board or upturned bowl. Leave 24 hours.

● Scribe three straight lines round the cake 2cm (¾ in), 3cm (1¼ in) and 4cm (1½ in) from the base.

● Prepare a large piping bag with no.57 petal tube (tip) and two colours of icing, see page 38. Using a steady pressure and slight shaking movement, pipe the frill against the lower scribed line. Pipe a second frill against the middle line and finally a third frill against the

upper line. Leave to dry.

● Attach the cake, still on its card, to the cake board with a dab of royal icing.

● Trace the inscription on page 38 and scribe onto cake top. Pipe using a no.1 tube (tip) and blue royal icing as shown in the step-by-step instructions on Piped Embroidery, page 39. Using the patterns and no.1 tubes (tips) with yellow and blue icing, pipe the embroidery on the cake top.

● Fix the ornament in place with a dab of royal icing.

EXPERT ADVICE
≈

Some shapes are just not appropriate for coating in royal icing and this cushion shape is one of them. Whilst it would be possible to achieve a smooth coating by softening the royal icing and pouring it over, this would result in a very hard-setting icing which would be difficult to cut and unpleasant to eat. Bake the cake in a large roasting tin (pan) or trim an oblong cake to shape.

Embroidery is usually piped freehand but if you wish you can trace the pattern and, using a scriber, pin-prick the main elements of the design onto the cake first. Make sure the subsequent piping covers the pinholes.

~ 1 ~

~ 2 ~

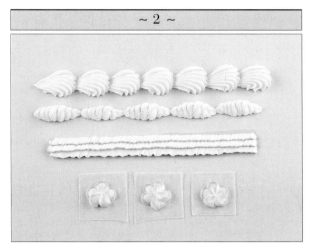

Using two colours in one piping bag can produce some spectacular effects. Piped borders are given additional emphasis and piped flowers and frills can be given subtle hints of colour. First use a narrow palette knife to wipe the coloured icing up one side of the piping bag.

Add the main colour, trying not to disturb the coloured stripe. Place the piping tube (tip) so that the colour will emerge in position (thin part of the petal tube for colour on an outside edge), then pipe until the effect emerges. Full peak icing is best.

Inscription and embroidery

~ ❖ ~

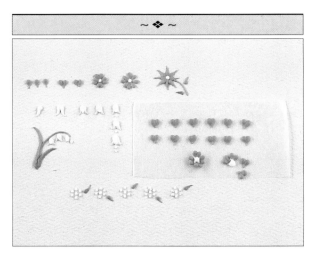

PIPED EMBROIDERY *The technique for piping tiny plain shells can be adapted to produce flowers and bells. Use a no.1 or 2 tube (tip). Piping can be done on wax paper or directly onto the cake surface.*

~ ❖ ~

Small writing tubes (tips) are all you need. This uses tiny bulbs, dots and shells. Use a scratched line technique on long curves and lines as this gives a more delicate finish that the 'touch, lift and drop' method. Several colours may be used for emphasis.

~ ❖ ~

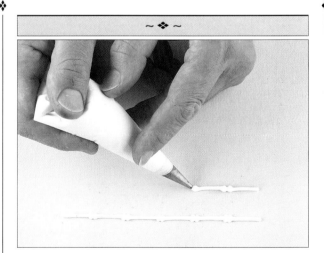

A bamboo effect is piped using a plain tube (tip) no. 1, 2 or 3. Pipe a short line; maintaining the same pressure, push the tip into the icing and pull out. Repeat to create the ridges typical of bamboo. Pipe another straight section and a ridge at the end.

~ ❖ ~

Long and short stitch can be combined with running stitch to create 'embroidered' inscriptions. This is effective in a design such as the Welcome Baby cake on page 37 where the overall effect is of an embroidered cushion.

HAPPY NEW YEAR

*B*ring a touch of Hogmanay to New Year celebrations with this bell-shaped cake.

---

23 x 18cm (10 x 9 in) bell cake
apricot glaze
1.25kg (2½ lb) marzipan (almond paste)
1.25kg (2½ lb) Royal Icing, see page 8
30g (1 oz) red sugarpaste
selection of food colourings
blue frost dusting powder (petal dust/blossom tint)
EQUIPMENT
33 x 28cm (13 x 11 in) bell cake board
tracing paper
scriber
no.3 sable paintbrush
no.1, 2 and 3 piping tubes (tips)
about 1.5m (1½ yd) ribbon for cake
about 1m (1¼ yd) ribbon or paper banding for board edge

● Brush cake with apricot glaze and cover with marzipan (almond paste). Coat the cake with white royal icing, leaving a little icing over for the piped decoration. Coat the board when the final coat of icing is completed. Leave to dry.

● Scribe the design onto the cake top using the pattern below. Brush the background area with blue frost dusting powder. Pipe the mountains, following the instructions in the step on page 43 for Brush Embroidery.

● Roll out the red sugarpaste and cut a strip 23cm (9 in) long and 2.5cm (1 in) wide. Cut the ends at an angle and create a small fold in the centre. Pipe a plaid pattern of your choice, following the step-by-step instructions on page 42 for coloured Trellis, after fixing the strip to the cake top with a few dots of royal icing.

● Pipe the thistles onto the cake top, following the step-by-step instructions on page 43.

● Using a no.3 tube (tip) pipe a plain shell border at the base of the cake. With the same tube (tip) pipe a top border of alternating shells. Pipe a single line inside the top border with the no.3 tube (tip).

● Fix ribbon round cake sides. Trim board edge with ribbon or paper banding.

NOTE A bell shape can be cut from an oblong or square cake if a bell frame is not available.

Templates for thistle leaves

~ 1 ~

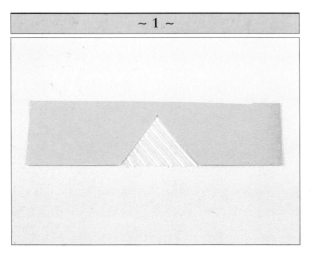

TWO-COLOUR TRELLIS *Give added impact to trellis piping by introducing colour. Scribe, or cut a template to outline the shape to be filled. Pipe the first row using no.2 tube (tip) and white icing. Add the colour with no.1 tube(tip), piping in between the first lines.*

~ 2 ~

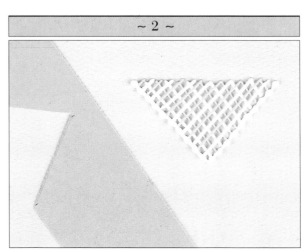

Pipe the cross pieces in the same order as the first stage. Remove the template, if used, and outline shape with linework or tiny plain shells.

~ 3 ~

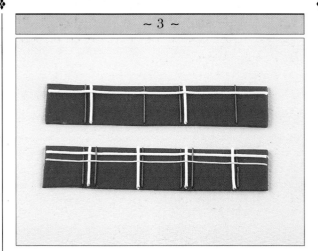

To pipe a tartan effect, cut a strip of red sugarpaste, fold if wished and position on cake or plaque. Have all bags of colour ready, using no.1 and 2 tubes (tips). Pipe the first stages as shown.

~ 4 ~

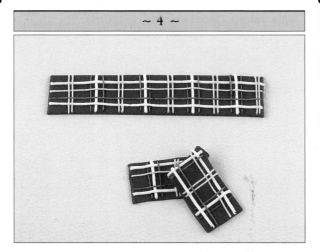

Add the subsequent colours and leave to dry. Experiment with your own colour combinations for different effects.

~ 1 ~

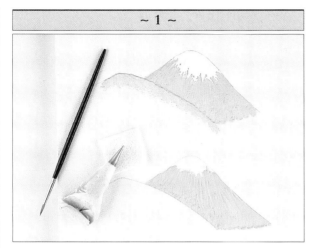

BRUSH EMBROIDERY MOUNTAINS *Adapt brush embroidery technique to create the mountains. Scribe the pattern onto the cake top. Turn cake around and pipe outline of distant mountain using green royal icing and no.3 piping tube (tip). Dampen no.3 sable paintbrush, squeeze between fingers to chisel shape and brush icing down. Leave rough. Turn cake right way round and pipe near slope and snow in the same way.*

~ 2 ~

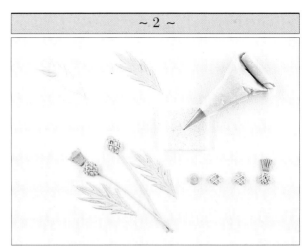

Using no.3 tube (tip) and green royal icing, pipe thistle stems. To form flower, pipe green bulb then, using no.1 tube (tip) and green icing, pipe lattice over this. Pipe small elongated bulbs in spaces. Using no.1 tube (tip) and heather colour, pipe outline of flower and fill in with zigzag motion. Overpipe with no.1 tube (tip) lines to represent characteristic thistle head. Outline each spike of leaves and brush down towards centre vein.

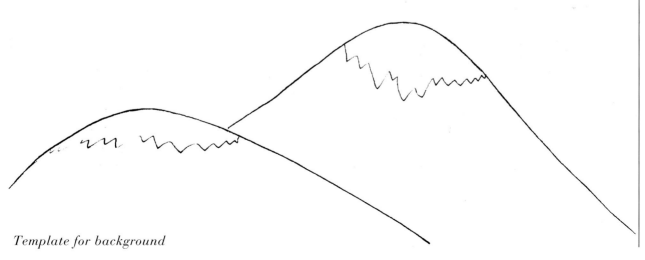

Template for background

'FLOATING' LACE AND FILIGREE CAKE

A teenage girl would feel very grown up if she were presented with a birthday cake like this. The archway and vesiculating linework suggest architectural stonework but the lace and clever 'floating' effect give the design lightness.

18cm (7 in) hexagonal cake
apricot glaze
1kg (2 lb) marzipan (almond paste)
1kg (2 lb) Royal Icing, see page 8
lilac food colouring
12 stencilled green leaves
6 stencilled flowers
EQUIPMENT
20cm (8 in) hexagonal cake card
15cm (6 in) round cake board
28cm (11 in) hexagonal cake board
tracing paper • scriber
no.1, 2 and 3 piping tubes (tips)
stencil paper • scalpel or craft knife
non-toxic adhesive • wax paper
1m (1¼ yd) ribbon or paper banding for board edge

● Brush cake with apricot glaze and cover with marzipan (almond paste). Centre the cake on the cake card and support on a smaller board or upturned bowl. Coat cake with pale lilac coloured icing, reserving some uncoloured icing for the decoration. Coat top and sides separately to achieve clean, square edges.

● Fix the round cake board to the hexagonal cake board using non-toxic adhesive and ensuring the round board is centrally placed. Coat the exposed part of the hexagonal board.

● Measure the coated cake, make a template of its shape and use this to scribe the outline on the coated hexagonal board. Trace and scribe the scroll pattern from the design on page 48 (or pipe this freehand if you wish). Also scribe a 5mm (¼ in) guideline, 2cm (¾ in) from each corner.

● At the edge of the round board, pipe bulbs with no.3 tube (tip) and pale lilac icing. Pipe a small tear-drop shape between each bulb with no.2 tube (tip) and pale lilac icing. With no.1 tube (tip) and deeper lilac icing, pipe a six-dot pattern along the scribed line which delineates the shape of the coated cake.

● Cut the pattern for the side linework (see page 70) from stencil paper. Centre the template on each side and scribe the design. Pipe the shape using no.2 tube (tip) and pale lilac icing then pipe a second line close to the first. With no.1 tube (tip) overpipe the first line using pale lilac icing. Finally, with deeper lilac and a no.1 tube (tip), pipe a third line inside the second and overpipe the first line. It will help to tilt the cake whilst you are carrying out this linework.

● Now fix the cake, on its card, to the round board using a strong, non-toxic adhesive.

● On the cake top, pipe built-up linework 2.5cm (1 in) in from the cake edge. The first row is piped with no.3 tube (tip) overpiped with a no.2 then no.1 tubes (tips), all in pale lilac. The second row, in pale lilac, is made using no.2 tube (tip) overpiped with no.1 tube (tip). The third row is pale lilac using no.1 tube (tip). Using no.1 tube (tip) and deeper lilac icing, overpipe the first and third rows, add a fourth row then finish with a scratched scallop line inside the fourth row.

● Pipe the lace flowers using the pattern on

page 48 and following the step-by-step instructions opposite for Piped Lace. You will need 54 flowers plus spares for breakages. Using the pattern on page 48, pipe the lace pieces for the cake base. You will need 36 pieces plus extra for breakages. Select appropriate numerals from the patterns on page 48 and make runouts in pale lilac, following the instructions on page 10. When the runouts are dry, pipe filigree over the top using no.1 tube (tip) and deep lilac icing. Embellish the edges of the numerals with pale lilac microdots in a three-dot sequence then pipe a deeper lilac dot between each sequence.

With no.1 tube (tip) and pale lilac icing, pipe the filigree linework between the top and side linework. Unlike cornelli work, which is based on embroidery, this vesiculating linework does touch – it is an imitation of stone-carving often seen on old buildings.

Fix the numerals in place on the cake top using a few dots of royal icing.

Between the top linework and the cake edge pipe a line using no.2 tube (tip) and pale lilac icing. At the angle of each corner pipe a small bulb. Fix the lace flowers in position at an angle against this piped line, securing them with a small, pale lilac bulb at the base of each, piped with no.1 tube (tip).

On the outer line of the side linework and 5mm (¼ in) above the cake base, pipe an inverted heart shape using no.3 tube (tip) and pale lilac icing. Fix the lace pieces at an angle at the base of side panels. Using no.1 tube (tip) and pale lilac icing, pipe a dot adjoining the base of each lace piece and an inverted tear-drop shape in between each piece.

On each of the six sides pipe the scroll pattern at the board edge, using no.1 tubes (tips) with pale and deep lilac icing.

Pipe dropped lines from the heart-shaped bulbs to the points scribed 2cm (¾ in) from each corner of the board. Use a no.2 tube (tip) and pale lilac icing. When that is dry, overpipe with no.1 tube (tip) and pale lilac, then finally no.1 tube (tip) and deeper lilac icing.

At each corner, position two green leaves, each 2cm (¾ in) in from the board edge and 1cm (½ in) in from the dropped line. Fix stencilled flowers in position with a small bulb of icing.

Trim the board edge with ribbon or paper banding.

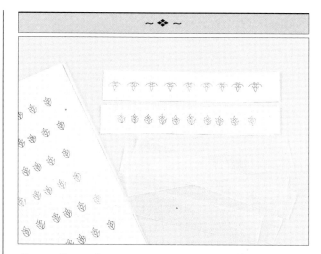

PIPED LACE *Lace patterns are usually drawn in sheets but a strip of wax paper fixed over one line of lace designs is easier to handle and saves copying. The sheet patterns can be covered with wax paper or slipped into a plastic wallet.*

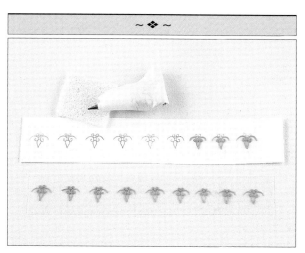

Pipe lace using a no.0 or 1 tube (tip). First paddle the royal icing well to remove air bubbles, then strain it through very fine mesh such as a piece of stocking material. Pipe the pattern in any way that feels comfortable for you.

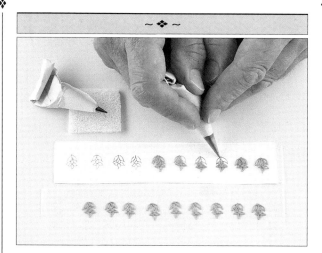

Lace in two or more colours is more difficult but very effective. Colour the icing with powder colours and prepare all bags before commencing work. Store lace flat in a dry place.

For general work lace may be attached to a line piped on the cake but for competition, fix by means of two or three tiny dots of icing. Ensure that all lace pieces are fixed at the same angle. Always pipe plenty of spare pieces to allow for breakages.

Template for scroll piping on board   *6-dot pattern*

Two-colour lace pattern, make 54 pieces

Lace at base border, make 36 pieces

Numbers
Also required for Child's Birthday Cake, see page 49 and 50th Birthday, see page 58.
Enlarge by 200% on a photocopier for Lace and Filigree Cake and Child's Birthday Cake;
use as shown for 50th Birthday

12345
67890

CHILD'S BIRTHDAY CAKE

*J*olly clowns are always a favourite with children. Here two novelty-piped figures hold the important birthday numeral between them.

23cm (9 in) round cake
apricot glaze
1.25k (2½ lb) marzipan (almond paste)
1.25kg (2½ lb) Royal Icing, see page 8
selection of food colourings
EQUIPMENT
30cm (12 in) round cake board
15cm (6 in) round cake board
stencil paper
no.1, 2, 3 and 13 piping tubes (tips)
6cm (2½ in) round pastillage plaque
wax paper for runouts
'Happy Birthday' stencil (optional)
about 1.25m (1⅓ yd) ribbon or paper banding
for board edge

Brush the cake with apricot glaze and cover with marzipan (almond paste). Coat with yellow-coloured royal icing, reserving a little icing uncoloured for the decorations. Coat the splay on the board when the final coat is completed.

Cut a stencil paper template 19cm (7½ in) diameter for the top and a strip of stencil paper the length of the circumference and 2.5cm (1 in) less than the depth of the cake. Fix the strip round the side of the cake, securing with masking tape. Place the circle template centrally on top of cake and anchor with 15cm (6 in) round cake board. Now stipple the exposed area following the instructions on page 20 for Side Designs and Flanges.

Using a no.13 piping tube (tip) pipe rosettes round the cake base.

Make three runout sea-lions and three jugglers, using the patterns below and overleaf, and following the step-by-step instructions on page 50. Make a runout numeral, using the pattern on page 48.

Stencil or pipe inscription on pastillage plaque. Using no.2 piping tubes (tips) pipe a border of plain shells in alternating colours of red, white and blue royal icing.

Following the step-by-step instructions on page 50, pipe two clowns, omitting a right arm on one and left arm on the other. When dry, position on top of cake with runout numeral supported by a small block of foam sponge between them. Pipe the remaining arms and hands to support the numeral. When dry, remove foam sponge support.

Fix plaque in position using small bulbs of icing. Fix sea-lions and acrobats round sides. Using multi-coloured icings in small bags cut at the end to the size of a no.1 tube (tip), pipe small bulbs round each juggler's upper body.

Trim board with ribbon or paper banding.

Juggler, make 3

~ 1 ~

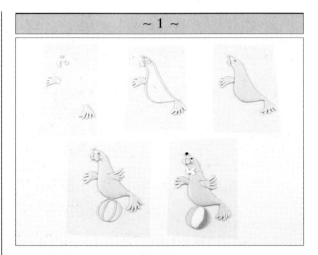

The sea-lions are run out in grey icing with the ball in multi-colours. Using the pattern on this page, on wax paper outline the figure and flood in in the order shown.

~ 2 ~

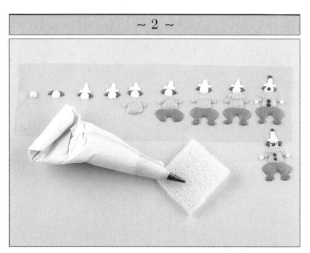

The juggling figures are not outlined so use a slightly thicker royal icing. Prepare small bags of your chosen colours, cutting the tip off when ready to pipe. Build up figure in the order shown, allowing each stage to crust over before piping the next

~ 3 ~

Novelty piping can be used to creat fun figures. Using well-beaten royal icing and no.1, 2 and 3 tubes (tips), pipe on the cake or on wax paper in the order shown. Several colours were used in one bag for the body. Keep tip of tube in icing as you pipe. Dry body before piping head.

Sealion, make 3

BASKETS OF ROSES

*M*any parents of present-day brides and grooms remember their own wedding cakes being decorated with raised trellis shapes and filigree – a popular style of decoration in the 1960s and 1970s. This modern design echoes that raised trellis in its delicate icing baskets.

23cm (9 in) round cake
15cm (6 in) round cake
10cm (4 in) round cake
2kg (4 lb) marzipan (almond paste)
apricot glaze
2kg (4 lb) Royal Icing, see page 8
pink and green food colourings
white vegetable fat (shortening) for greasing moulds

E Q U I P M E N T
36cm (14 in) round cake board
25cm (10 in) round cake board
18cm (7 in) round cake board
moulds for baskets
no.1, 2, 3, 43, 44 and 56 piping tubes (tips)
tracing paper
scriber
three 9cm (3½ in) pink cake pillars
three 7.5cm (3 in) pink cake pillars
about 2.5m (2¾ yd) ribbon or paper banding for board edge
top ornament of silk flowers

● Brush the cakes with apricot glaze and cover with marzipan (almond paste). Coat the cakes with pale pink royal icing, coating the boards when the final coat has been completed.

● Following the step-by-step instructions on page 54, make piped baskets – five for the base tier, six each for the middle and top – not forgetting some spares in case of breakages. Adjust the templates for the basket tops, on page 68, if necessary, and make a top for each basket. Make about 150 piped roses and buds, following the step-by-step instructions shown on page 28.

● **BASE TIER:** Cut a template for the cake top design, using the pattern on page 68 and scribe onto cake top. Mark the positions of the pillars, outlining the shape with no.2 piping tube (tip) and pale pink icing. Pipe top linework using no.3 and no.2 piping tubes (tips). The three rows are piped as follows:- no.3 overpiped with no.3; no.3 overpiped with no.2; no.2.

● Cut a template for the side of the cake, fold into six and cut the pattern shown on page 68, adjusting shape of basket and length of swags if necessary. Fix template round side and scribe design, ensuring that pattern is aligned with top linework. At front section of cake, upturn template and scribe the large top curve to create the area for the monogram. Trace monogram initials from alphabet on page 67 and scribe only the outline onto cake.

● Tilt cake slightly and pipe short swags and bells using no.3 piping tube (tip) and pale pink royal icing.

● Pipe monogram outlines using no.2 tube (tip) and pale pink icing. Pipe trellis lines across each letter using no.1 tube (tip) and deep pink royal icing, keeping the line raised away from the cake surface. Overpipe the outlines of the letters, and the ends of the trellis lines, with the same tube (tip). Pipe plain shell outline to monogram area using no.2 tube (tip).

● Pipe base and top borders using pale pink royal icing and no.44 tube (tip). Overpipe a reverse 'S' line using no.3 tube (tip).

~ 1 ~

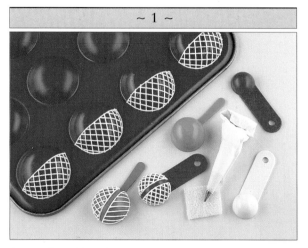

Raised trellis shapes may be piped on lightly greased moulds. Use a white fat to grease the mould – bun tins (muffin pans) and measuring spoons are ideal. Using no.2 piping tube (tip) and royal icing, pipe the outline then fill in with trellis.

~ 2 ~

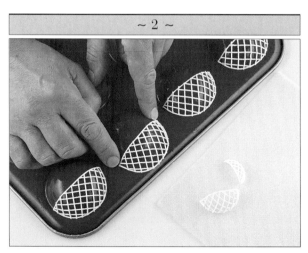

When the trellis is dry, warm the mould in a gentle heat and the piped shape will release with a slight push.

~ 3 ~

Fix these baskets to the cake by piping a line of royal icing around the edge which meets the cake, using a no.2 piping tube (tip). Hold basket up to cake and gently push into place. Neaten edge, and make secure, by piping a line of plain shells round edge with no.2 tube (tip).

~ 4 ~

Have ready template of basket top; place wax paper over template, pipe outline then fill in with zigzag piping using no.2 tube (tip). When dry fix in place on basket top with line of royal icing. Fix flowers and foliage in place.

MIDDLE TIER: Make top and side templates as for base tier but omitting space for monogram. Pipe side linework using no.2 piping tube (tip). Top linework is no.3 tube (tip) overpiped with no.2 tube (tip), with no.2 tube (tip) line piped inside the first. Borders are piped with no.44 tube (tip) overpiped with no.3 tube (tip).

TOP TIER: Make top and side templates as for previous tier. Pipe side linework using no.2 piping tube (tip). Top linework is a single line piped with no.2 tube (tip). Borders are piped with no.43 tube (tip), overpiped with no.2 tube (tip).

Following the step-by-step instructions on page 54, fix baskets and tops to cakes and fill with roses, securing flowers with small bulbs of icing. Pipe fern effect using no.1 piping tube (tip) and green royal icing. Using a small piping bag cut to a 'V' at the end, pipe leaves amongst the roses.

Using no.1 tube (tip) pipe a scalloped line around the edge of each board.

Trim boards with ribbon or paper banding.

EXPERT ADVICE

≈

Plaster cake pillars complement royal icing particularly well because their surface texture is similar to that of the icing. In addition, they may be coloured to match tinted icing. Use non-toxic water paints and avoid painting the bottom of the pillar which is in contact with the icing.

DESIGNING RUNOUT PANELS AND COLLARS

*P*atterns for runout off-pieces and collars are available in many source books but they do not always fit exactly since cake tins (pans) vary in size and the thicknesses of marzipan (almond paste) and icing can be different from one cake to another. When this happens, or when you want to create an exclusive design, then it is important to know how to draw runout panels and collars.

Exact measurements and accurate drawing are paramount if the finished runout is to fit your cake neatly. For all special work, marzipan (almond paste) and coat the cake before you start drawing, this way your runout will look tailor-made for your cake and, where panels are involved, there will be no problems fitting the pieces together.

EQUIPMENT
A3 size sheets cartridge paper
ruler
HB pencils
coloured pencil (crayon)
pencil eraser
90° set square
pair of compasses
pencil sharpener
protractor (optional)

SIDE PANELS These are an effective method of enhancing or disguising the shape of a cake. Panels can be used to enclose the sides completely, see 50th Birthday Cake, page 58, or to provide decoration on part of the sides, see Good Luck Cake, page 60 and Anniversary Cake, page 62.

FLAT PANELS ON FLAT-SIDED CAKE Measure depth of coated cake. If panel is to stand on a base runout, allow about 2mm (⅛ in) for the thickness of that runout. Note the measurement. Measure length of cake sides. Draw a plan of cake. Round this draw the cake board. If the panels are to decorate part of the side, decide on their position (placed centrally or abutting at corners) and distance from side of cake – they may be fixed against the cake side or placed at a distance. Draw a line to represent length of panel; note the measurement.

These two measurements, height and width, may now be used to draw the outline of the panel and your chosen design can be drawn within that area.

The plan of the cake may be used as a basis for designing top and base runouts.

FLAT PANELS ON ROUND CAKE Measure depth of coated cake. If panel is to stand on a base runout, allow about 2mm (⅛ in) for the thickness of that runout. Note the measurement.

Measure diameter of coated cake. On cartridge paper, draw a circle this size. This circle is known as the cake line and is usually shown in illustrations as a broken or dotted line. If you use a coloured pencil to draw this line it will save confusion later.

Measure the cake board. Using the same centre point as for the cake line, draw a circle to represent the cake board.

Using drawing instruments, divide the cake line into the required number of sections (usually 6 or 8). Placing a ruler on the circle so that two opposite divisions and the centre are aligned, draw faint guidelines from the cake line towards the board edge. Repeat for all divisions.

Bisect one division as shown below.

Where the dividing line crosses the cake line, draw a line at right angles, extending it so that it meets the two guidelines on either side. This line represents the length of the runout panel. When completed, the panel will touch the cake side at the centre point. Note the measurement and use with the figure for the depth of the cake to draw the outline of the panel. Your chosen design may be drawn within that area.

Bisecting an angle

With compass point at (a) and set at at least half the distance between (a) and (b), describe an arc outside the circle. Repeat, with the same compass setting, from point (b). A line drawn from the centre of the circle to point (c) will bisect the angle.

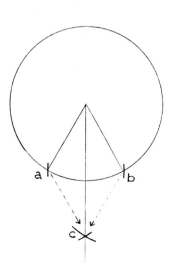

Flat panel on flat-sided cake

Line (a) – (b) is length of panel

Flat panel on round cake

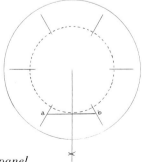

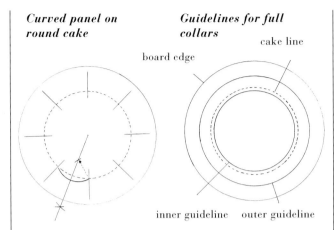

Curved panel on round cake

Guidelines for full collars

board edge

cake line

inner guideline   outer guideline

CURVED PANELS These may be the entire depth of the cake or cover only parts of it, see Anniversary Cake, page 62.

Draw a plan of the cake and board as described previously. Divide the cake line into the required number of sections. Bisect one of the sections.

Set the compasses at the width which corresponds to the curve on which you intend to dry the panels, for example if you are using 10cm (4 in) guttering, set the compasses at 5cm (2 in).

Put the compass point at the junction between the cake line and one of the dividing lines and make an arc to cross the bisecting line on the inside of the circle. Re-position the compass point at this junction and draw a curve between the two dividing lines.

The length of the curve can be calculated mathematically but a practical method is to stand the chosen drying mould on the drawing, mark the ends of the curve on the mould in pencil then measure the distance between the pencil marks with a tape measure or string. This is the base measurement of the design; use this to draw the panel pattern.

OFF-PIECES AND FULL COLLARS Draw a plan of the cake top and board.

Draw guidelines for the outside and inside edges of the runout. The inside edge needs to overlap the cake edge by about 5mm (3⁄16 in). The distance from this to the outside edge will vary depending on the size of the cake, from 2.5cm (1 in) for an 18cm (6 in) cake to 3.8cm (1½ in) for a 25cm (10 in) cake. Let your eye guide you and remember it is possible to have some areas of the runout extending beyond the guidelines. The important thing is that the outermost part of the runout is protected by the cake board, so allow a board 7.5 – 10cm (3 – 4 in) larger than the cake.

Decide on a full collar or sections, divide the circles accordingly and draw the runout within the guidelines.

A base collar or section does not require an overlap; measure the diameter of the cake and use that as the guideline for the inside edge of the runout. Base collars or sections should be slightly wider than the top runout in order to achieve a balanced design.

All drawings may be photocopied to give accurate working drawings from which to produce the runouts of the circle.

EXPERT ADVICE

≈

To check if an existing design will fit your cake, or to double-check your own drawings, trace the runout design onto greaseproof paper and cut it out, then try the pattern against the coated cake; any adjustment necessary to make the runout fit will then be evident.

50th BIRTHDAY

*D*isguise a round cake with runout panels to create this hexagonal box. The runout collar is fixed at only three or four points so that it can be lifted off easily when the cake is portioned.

18cm (7 in) round cake ● apricot glaze
750g (1½ lb) marzipan (almond paste)
1kg (2 lb) Royal Icing, see page 8
selection of food colourings
EQUIPMENT
28cm (11 in) round cake board ● tracing paper
cartridge paper ● wax paper for runouts
scriber ● no.1, 2 and 3 piping tubes (tips)
about 1m (1 yd) ribbon or paper banding for
board edge

● Brush the cake with apricot glaze and cover with marzipan (almond paste). Coat with pale grey royal icing, reserving some uncoloured for the decorations. Coat the cake board when the final coat of icing is completed.

● Check the runout collar and panel designs on page 70 against the coated cake for size (see Designing Panels and Collars, page 55); adjust size if necessary then make one collar and six panels. Using the patterns on page 69, make the runout yacht sections and six sets of numerals.

● Pipe alternating pale and dark grey dots round the inside edge of the runout panels using no.1 piping tube (tip). At the sides of each panel, pipe straight lines in pale green using no.2 tube (tip). Pipe a pale grey no.1 line next to this. Using no.1 tube (tip) and deep grey icing, overpipe the no.2 line and pipe a line inside the other two.

● Using no.2 tube (tip) and medium grey royal icing, pipe a continuous line of plain shells round the centre of the cake side and the base.

● On the runout collar, pipe a continuous line of plain shells round the inside edge, using a no.2 tube (tip) and pale grey icing. Pipe the graduated bulb embellishment with the same tube, then pipe alternating deep and pale grey dots round the outside edge, using no.2 tube.

● Fix panels in place, securing with bulbs of royal icing at each bottom corner and at centre top. Continue the linework on each panel to the edge of the cake board as shown. Pipe alternating pale and dark grey bulbs at the base of each panel and along the join between panels, using no.2 piping tube (tip). With the same tubes (tips) pipe the scrollwork pattern on the board. With small bulbs of icing, fix the numerals in place centred in the 'window' of each panel.

● Free the top collar from the runout paper. Keeping it on the paper, position collar on cake top then gently slide paper out at one side, taking care not to damage the panels. Secure with three or four bulbs of icing between underside and panels.

● Fix the runout yacht pieces in place and pipe in mast, pennant, and linework using white royal icing and no.2 tube (tip). Put some blue and white royal icing into the same piping bag, cut off the end of the bag to the size of a no.3 tube (tip) and pipe the waves beneath the yacht. Using medium grey royal icing and no. 1 tube (tip) pipe the inscription and linework on cake top.

● Inside the runout collar, pipe a line in pale grey icing using no.3 tube (tip). Overpipe with no.2 tube (tip), then pipe alternating pale and deep grey dots inside this line.

● Trim board edge with ribbon or banding.

GOOD LUCK CAKE

*C*ranes are a Japanese symbol representing happiness and prosperity and the central motif in this design is taken from a Chinese symbol for good luck.

18cm (7 in) square cake
apricot glaze
750g (1½ lb) marzipan (almond paste)
875g (1¾ lb) Royal Icing, see page 8
EQUIPMENT
28cm (11 in) square cake board
tracing paper
4 oval pastillage plaques
8.5cm (3¼ in) round pastillage plaque
no.1 and 2 piping tubes (tips)
non-toxic gold food colouring
about 1.25m (1 yd) ribbon or paper banding
for board edges

● Brush the cake with apricot glaze and cover with marzipan (almond paste). Coat with royal icing, coating the cake board when the final coat of icing is completed.

● Check the runout panel and off-piece designs on page 69/70 against the coated cake for size (see Designing Panels and Collars, page 55); adjust size if necessary then make four base corner pieces and four top corner pieces. Make eight panels by first piping the frame area (shown shaded in the design). When that is dry, centre the panel over the design and pipe the flower and leaf design using no.2 piping tube (tip) and a bag cut to a 'V' shape at the end for the leaves.

● Using the patterns on page 70, make a runout of the top centrepiece and pipe four cranes. When these are dry, paint with non-

toxic gold food colour and fix to plaques with a little royal icing. Fix centrepiece plaque in place using small bulbs of royal icing.

● Remove base corner runouts from paper and fix in position using small bulbs of royal icing. Pipe bamboo pattern between corner pieces at base of cake, using no.2 tube (tip) and following the step-by-step instructions on page 39 for Piped Flowers and Embroidery. Fix crane plaques in position on the centre sides, using small bulbs of royal icing.

● To fix the side panels, pipe three bulbs of royal icing, using no.2 tube (tip), on the side of the cake at the top edge. Peel the paper from a panel, stand it in position on a base cornerpiece and press lightly against the piped bulbs – these should secure the panel at the top as well as holding it slightly proud of the cake surface. Fix an adjacent panel in the same way then pipe bamboo pattern at the base and at the junction of the two panels. Repeat for other three sides.

● Position the top cornerpieces, fixing them with a line of royal icing piped on the top edge of the cake. Pipe linework inside the cornerpieces, as illustrated, using no.2 and no.1 tubes (tips).

● Trim the board edge with ribbon or paper banding.

NOTE: Whilst gold food colouring is non-toxic, it is not edible. Be sure to give instructions that the plaques be removed from the cake before it is cut and eaten.

Pattern for piped crane, make 4

ANNIVERSARY CAKE

*T*his design lends itself to adaptation for many occasions simply by changing the colour scheme or inscription.

two 20cm (8 in) round cakes
apricot glaze
1.25k (2½ lb) marzipan (almond paste)
1.5k (3 lb) Royal Icing, see page 8
selection of food colourings

E Q U I P M E N T

33cm (13 in) round cake board
36cm (14 in) round cake board
non-toxic adhesive
tracing paper
cartridge paper
wax paper for runouts
curved former for drying runouts
no.1, 2 and 3 piping tubes (tips)
'Congratulations' stencil (optional)
about 2.25m (2½ yd) ribbon or paper banding
for board edge

● Join the two cakes to form one deep cake as shown in the step-by-step instructions on page 15. Using non-toxic adhesive, stick the two cake boards together.

● Brush the cake with apricot glaze and cover with marzipan (almond paste). Coat the cake with terra-cotta coloured royal icing. When the final coat of icing is completed, coat the cake board and the exposed area of the larger board.

● Check the runout panel and off-piece designs on page 62 against the coated cake for size (see Designing Panels and Collars, page 55); adjust size if necessary then make eight off-pieces for the base border and eight off-pieces for the top border. Make eight curved pieces for each of the top and base borders; pipe and flood in each piece on a flat board using runout icing just sufficiently soft to flow, filling in the shape from the centre to the edges. Transfer the runout to the curved drying form and dry the pieces as quickly as possible.

● Make a template for the side design, using the pattern on page 71. Hold the template in place with masking tape. Pipe the 'dot and dash' side linework just below the template then remove the template carefully. Stencil or pipe the inscription on the cake top.

● On the outside edges of all the off-pieces, pipe a six-dot picot edge with a brown dot between each set, using no.1 piping tube (tip). On the inside edge of the top border pieces, using no.1 tubes (tips) and terra-cotta and brown royal icing, pipe the reverse 'S' and 'C' border design.

● Using no.3 piping tube (tip) and terra-cotta coloured icing, pipe the 'fleur-de-lys' design at the junction of the linework swags on the cake side.

● Following the step-by-step instructions on page 64, position the raised base off-pieces, taking care to line them up with the side linework. Using no.3 tube (tip) pipe a line of plain shells where the off-pieces and the cake meet. Pipe the 'fleur-de-lys' design between the off-pieces on the board using no.3 tube (tip) and terra-cotta icing and a no.1 tube (tip) and brown icing.

● Fix the curved base panels, following the step-by-step instructions on page 64. Using a no.1 piping tube (tip), pipe a plain shell border round the base of each panel and at the junction of each two panels. Pipe the scroll design round the board edge using no.1 tubes (tips) and terra-cotta and brown royal icing.

Pipe a line down each side of a curved top panel and set in place very slightly under the top edge of the cake, aligning the piece with the side linework. Secure to cake with piped shells down each side, using no.1 tube (tip).

Fix the top off-pieces in position above each curved panel, using a few dots of royal icing. Using no.3 piping tube (tip) pipe a bulb at the joins of the pieces. With terra-cotta icing and no.3 tube (tip), pipe a line inside the top sections; overpipe with no.1 tube (tip) and pipe a line inside the first. Using no.1 tube (tip) and brown royal icing, pipe a third line inside the other two.

Trim both cake board edges with ribbon or paper banding. With no.3 tube (tip) and terra-cotta icing, pipe a plain shell border at the join between the cake boards.

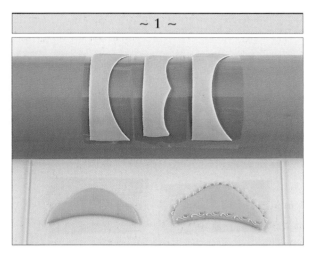

~ 1 ~

New plastic guttering and drainpipe make ideal formers for drying curved runout sections.

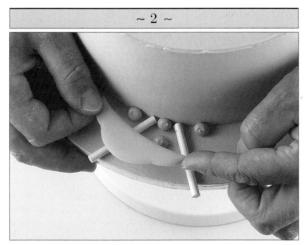

~ 2 ~

To create a raised border of runout sections, pipe bulbs of royal icing, place pieces of dowelling in position, then lower runout section into place. Remove dowelling when icing has set.

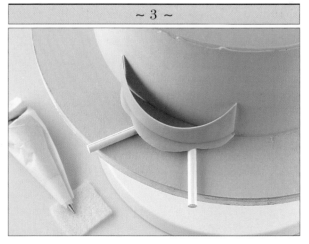

~ 3 ~

Pipe a line of royal icing along each side of the curved base section then carefully position, making contact with the cake side. Secure in place with shells or bulbs.

Cake decorating is one of those crafts which easily develops into a small business from a hobby. This change sometimes occurs almost unnoticed as a decorator gains a reputation and gradually finds that, as well as family and friends, complete strangers are ordering special cakes.

If these orders expand to the extent that the decorator is producing cakes for a period of five days in any five consecutive weeks, then the 'business' will come within the Food Premises Registration Regulations 1991, which require all food businesses to register their premises with the local authority.

Whether registered or not, any food business falls within the Food Safety Act 1990 and may be visited by an Environmental Health Officer (EHO) who is empowered to ensure that the premises and equipment fall within the regulations.

If your hobby reaches a stage where it seems to be turning into a business it is a good idea to contact your local EHO and request an advisory visit so that you can make any alterations to your kitchen before the business is formally launched.

Although the Food Safety Act 1990 does not cover food prepared at home for consumption in the home, it does make it an offence to sell any food which fails to meet safety requirements – even at charity fund-raising events. So it is sensible to ensure that your kitchen or workroom is clean, in good condition, well lit and ventilated. You should have plenty of hot and cold water and a hand wash basin separate from the sink for washing up. Do not have a lavatory or bedroom opening off the work area. Pets and pet food are not permitted in the room, nor personal laundry. Food must be protected from contamination. It is recommended that, as a 'food handler', you undergo training in basic food hygiene.

Engagement Cake, see page 18 Alphabet shown half size

Pipe the outline using a no.2 piping tube (tip), then pipe trellis using no.1 tube (tip). The trellis is always piped at an angle, but the angle may be varied so that two intertwined letters complement each other.

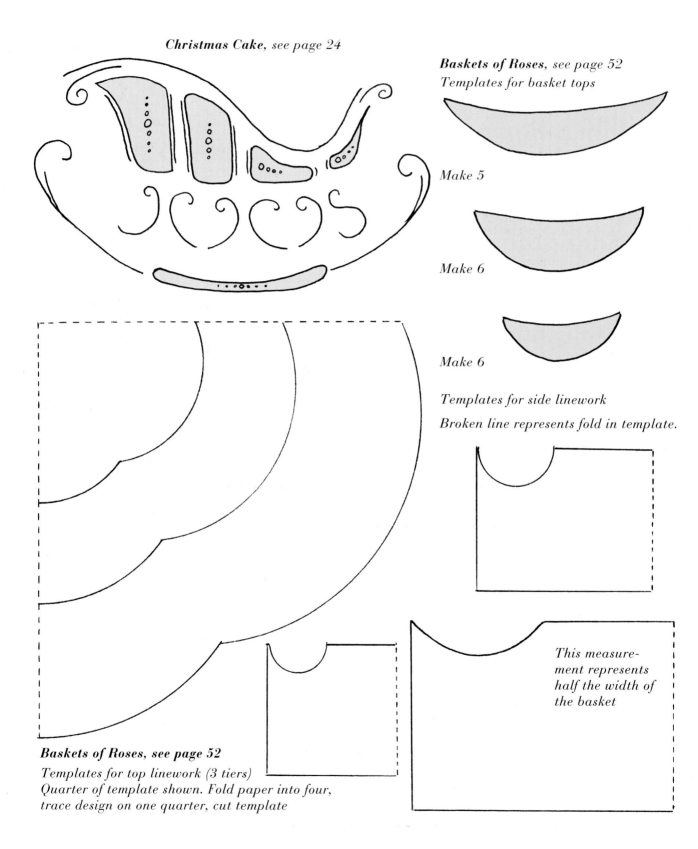

Christmas Cake, *see page 24*

Baskets of Roses, *see page 52*
Templates for basket tops

Make 5

Make 6

Make 6

Templates for side linework
Broken line represents fold in template.

*This measure-
ment represents
half the width of
the basket*

Baskets of Roses, *see page 52*

Templates for top linework (3 tiers)
Quarter of template shown. Fold paper into four,
trace design on one quarter, cut template

50th Birthday,
see page 58

Pattern for yacht motif

Template for base runouts, make 4

Template for top runouts, make 4

Good Luck,
see page 60

Congratulations

Template for inscriptions

Pattern for runout side panels, make 6

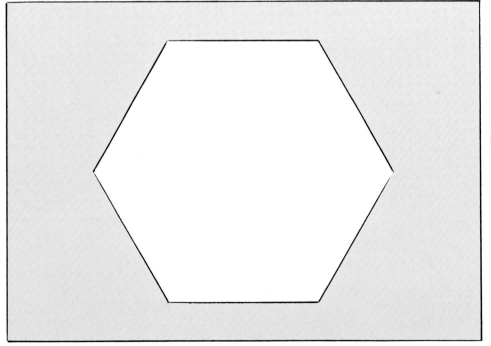

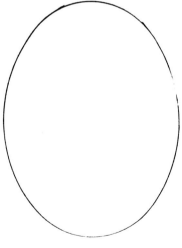

Template for side plaques – runout or cut from pastillage, make 4

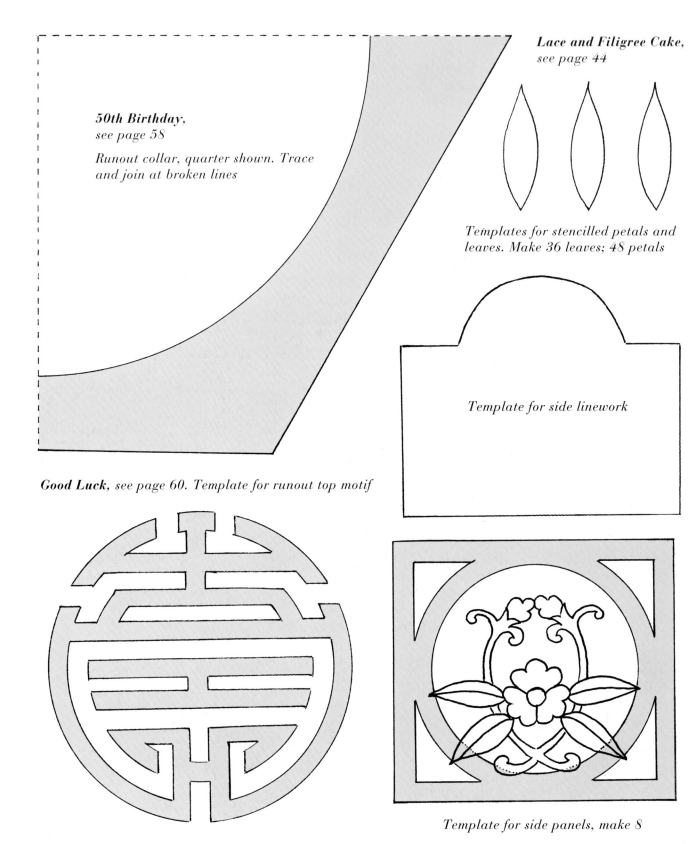

50th Birthday, see page 58

Runout collar, quarter shown. Trace and join at broken lines

Lace and Filigree Cake, see page 44

Templates for stencilled petals and leaves. Make 36 leaves; 48 petals

Template for side linework

Good Luck, see page 60. Template for runout top motif

Template for side panels, make 8

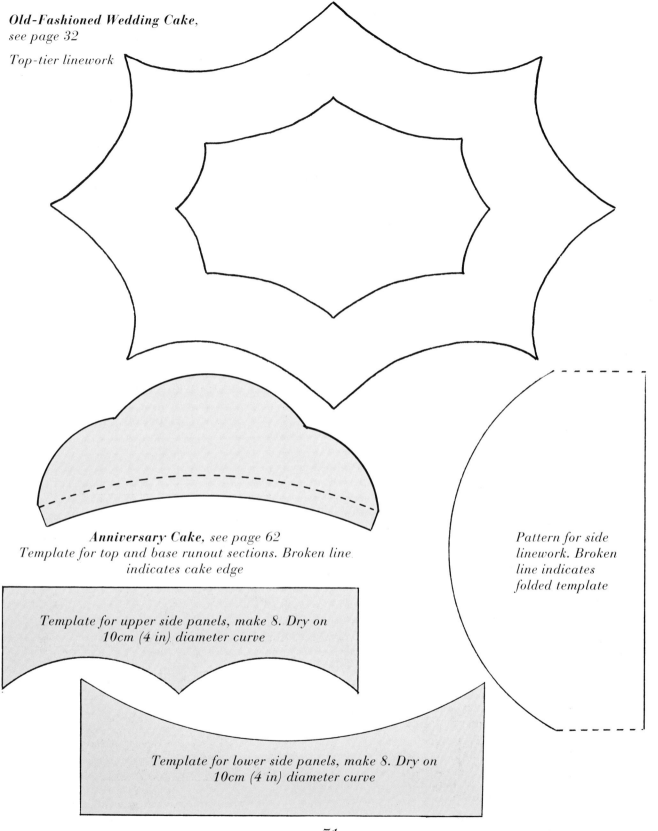

Old-Fashioned Wedding Cake,
see page 32

Top-tier linework

Anniversary Cake, *see page 62*
Template for top and base runout sections. Broken line indicates cake edge

Template for upper side panels, make 8. Dry on 10cm (4 in) diameter curve

Pattern for side linework. Broken line indicates folded template

Template for lower side panels, make 8. Dry on 10cm (4 in) diameter curve

INDEX

adding machine rolls 6, 15
albumen powder 8, 10
almond paste 16
alphabets 66
angles, bisecting 56 – 7
Anniversary Cake 62 – 4, 71

baking tins, shaped 14-16
bamboo effect 39
baskets 30 – 1
Baskets of Roses 52 – 5,
  67 – 8
bells 26
Birthday cakes:
  Child's Birthday Cake,
    49 – 51
  50th Birthday Cake 58,
    69 – 70
bisecting an angle 56 – 7
borders 18 – 20
brush embroidery 43

cake boards, hiding 21, 34
cake knives 6
caster sugar, dredging 26
Child's Birthday Cake 49 – 51
chocolate: rich truffles 17
Christening cakes 36 – 7
Christmas Cake 24 – 6, 68
clowns 49 – 51
coating consistency 9
collars, designing 56, 57
colours 10
  gold food colouring 60
  pillars 55
  piped lace 47
  piping two colours 38
comb scrapers 20, 23
consistency 9
cornflour 14

cranes, piped 60
curved panels 56, 57
curved runouts 64
cutting cakes 17, 21

dowels 6, 15, 16 – 17
drawing equipment 6
dredging caster sugar 26
drying runouts 11
dusting bags 14

electric mixers 6, 7
embroidery 38 – 9
Engagement Cake 18 – 20, 66
equipment 6

50th Birthday Cake 58 – 9,
  69 – 70
filigree work 46
flanges 22 – 3
flat panels 56
flooding 10 – 11
flowers, stencils 12
Food Safety Act (1990) 65
full peak consistency 9

gelatine 12
gold food colouring 60
Good Luck Cake 60 – 1, 69
grapes, piping 21
gum tragacanth 12

Happy New Year 40 – 1
heart-shaped cakes 16
holly 26
horseshoe-shaped cakes 16
hygiene 65

Keepsake Cake 27 – 31
knives 6, 17

lace, piping 47
Lace and Filigree Cake 44 – 6
linework, consistency 9
long and short stitch 39

marzipan 16
mats, runouts 11
meringue powder 8, 10
mixers, electric 6, 7
moulds 6, 13

New Year cake 40 – 1

Old-fashioned Wedding Cake
  32 – 5, 71

packaging cakes 17, 46
panels, designing 55 – 7
paper: runouts 11
  stencil 6
pastillage 12 – 14
petal-shaped cakes 16
petal tubes 27
pillars 17, 55
piping: bells 26
  embroidery 38 – 9
  grapes 21
  holly 26
  lace 47
  ribbon 30
  roses 28
  scratched line 46
  trellis 42
  two colours 38
raised borders 64
raised trellis shapes 54
rebeating 10
ribbon, piping 30
roses 28, 52 – 5, 67 – 8

royal icing, recipe 8 – 10
runouts 10 – 11
  curved 64
  designing panels 55 – 7
  icing consistency 9
  raised borders 64

Savoy bags and tubes 6
scalloped oval cakes 16
scrapers 6, 20, 23
scratched line piping 46
sea-lions 50
serrated scrapers 20
shaped cakes 14 – 16
side designs 20
side panels, designing 55 – 6
side scrapers 6, 20
stencil paper 6, 21
stencils 11 – 12
stippled icing 22
storage 10
striped icing 23

tartan effect 42
templates 21, 66 – 71
thinning icing 10
thistles 43
tiered cakes 16 – 17
till rolls 6, 15
trellis shapes 42, 54
truffles 17

wedding cakes:
  Basket of Roses 52 – 5,
    67 – 8
  Old-Fashioned 32 – 5, 71
Welcome Baby 36 – 7
writing consistency 9

FOR FURTHER INFORMATION

Merehurst is the leading publisher of cake decorating books and has an excellent range of titles to suit cake decorators of all levels. Please send for a free catalogue, stating the title of this book:

United Kingdom
Marketing Department
Merehurst Ltd.
Ferry House
51 -57 Lacy Road
London SW15 1PR
Tel: 081 780 1177
Fax: 081 780 1714

U.S.A./Canada
Foxwood International Ltd.
P.O. Box 267
145 Queen Street S.
Missisauga, Ontario
L5M 2BS Canada
Tel: (1) 416 567 4800
Fax: (1) 416 567 4681

Australia
J.B. Fairfax Ltd.
80 McLachlan Avenue
Rushcutters Bay
NSW 2011
Tel: (61) 2 361 6366
Fax: (61) 2 360 6262

Other Territories
For further information
contact:
International Sales
Department at United
Kingdom address.